W9-BXV-733

napkins with a twist

**Also by David Stark**

*To Have and To Hold: Magical Wedding Bouquets*
(coauthor with Avi Adler)

*Wild Flowers: Projects and Inspiration*
(coauthor with Avi Adler)

# napkins with a twist
fabulous folds with flair for every occasion

## david stark
with john morse
photographs by mick hales

ARTISAN    NEW YORK

Copyright © 2006 by David Stark

Photographs copyright © 2006 by Mick Hales,
excluding Additional Photo Credits below

Step-by-step photographs
copyright © 2006 by Arnold Katz Photography

The Coronation Fold, created to celebrate the
Golden Jubilee of HM Queen Elizabeth II
(1952–2002), The Throne Fold, created to
celebrate the fiftieth anniversary of the Queen's
coronation (1953–2003), and the Prince of
Wales Fold, created for and used at the wedding
of Prince Charles to Camilla Parker Bowles,
2005, are copyright © by Luigi Spotorno, their
designer.

Additional Photo Credits page 29, The
Greenbrier Fold, courtesy of The Greenbrier;
page 41, The Pierre Hotel Fold, courtesy of
The Pierre, a Taj Hotel; page 50, The Coronation
Fold, Topham/The Image Works; page 60,
The *Titanic* Fold, Getty Images/Getty Images;
page 66, The Prince of Wales Fold, Topham/
The Image Works; page 78, The Throne Fold,
Tim Graham/Corbis; page 101, The White
House Fold, courtesy of Workman Publishing;
page 105, The Restaurant Michel Bras Fold,
Christian Palis; page 109, The Delmonico's Fold,
courtesy of Delmonico's; page 113, The French
Laundry Fold, Deborah Jones/courtesy of The
French Laundry; page 123, The Kennedy White
House Fold, CBS Photo Archive/Getty Images.

All rights reserved. No portion of this
book may be reproduced—mechanically,
electronically, or by any means, including
photocopying—without written permission
of the publisher.

Published by Artisan
A Division of Workman Publishing, Inc.
225 Varick Street
New York, New York 10014
www.artisanbooks.com

*Library of Congress*
*Cataloging-in-Publication Data*
Stark, David, 1968–
Napkins with a twist : fabulous folds
with flair for any occasion / David Stark.
    p. cm.
ISBN-13: 978-1-57965-296-8
ISBN-10: 1-57965-296-4
1. Napkin folding.  I. Title.
TX879.S723 2006
642'.79—dc22          2005055868

Printed in China.

10 9 8 7 6 5 4 3 2 1

Book design by Nicholas Caruso

For my dad, who amused us no end with his endless doodles
of "bowling pin man" and "B" Lady on many a restaurant's napkin

# Contents

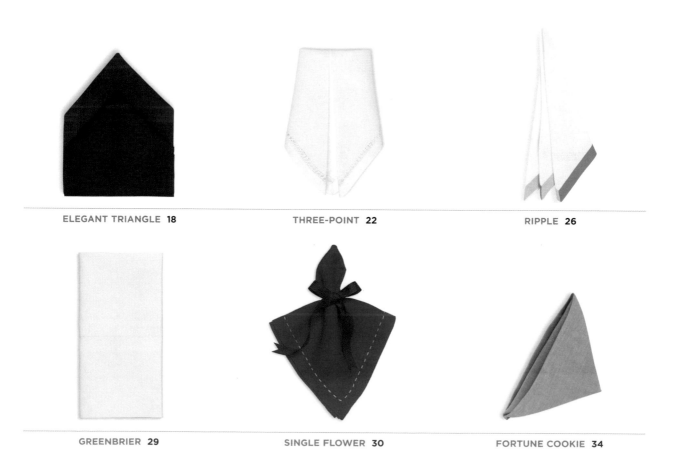

**ELEGANT TRIANGLE 18**    **THREE-POINT 22**    **RIPPLE 26**

**GREENBRIER 29**    **SINGLE FLOWER 30**    **FORTUNE COOKIE 34**

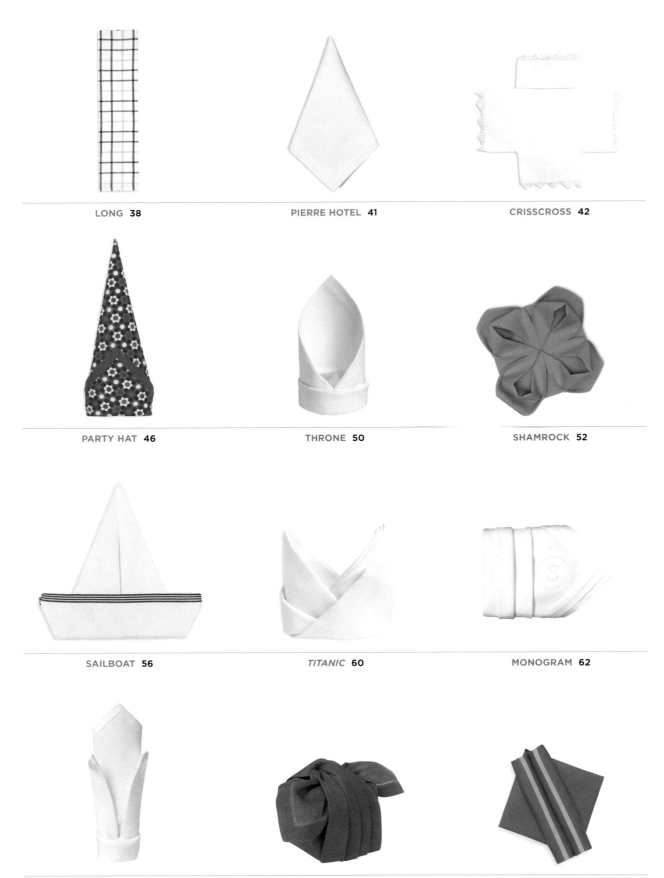

Bon Appétit!

# Introduction

It's often said that what makes life special is "the little things." That's what napkin folding is: a little extra effort that transforms an everyday nothing, such as a napkin, into a splendid something, a gift just waiting to be unwrapped.

An elegantly folded napkin is a harbinger of good things to come, the invitation to a wonderful epicurean adventure, the promise of thoughtfulness and whimsy. It signals a celebration.

When guests take their seats, their napkins are the first thing they see, the first thing they touch, and the first and last item they use. The napkin—and by extension, its presentation—matters.

Nothing dresses up a place setting like a smartly folded napkin. The "china" may be Melmac, but add a clever napkin fold and suddenly the dinner takes on a whole new pizzazz, becoming a place setting with sparkle and a meal set into motion.

A delicious fold runs from a plain rectangle of linen folded three times to a dazzling confection specifically tailored for the occasion. There are the joy and rewards you find in expanding your cuisine, and you'll also find them in dressing up your place settings—starting with your napkins. If you're willing to go through the intricacies of preparing an extraordinary five-course meal (or even if your goal is simply to make a night of Chinese takeout something special), don't take a shortcut when landscaping your table.

I've made a career out of taking the so-called mundane things of life and turning them into fun and important players. And so I do it with napkins. Something normally taken for granted is given the right attention, and it becomes the cherry on top of the sundae.

A high priority for my clients is making the most of their entertainment budget. But regardless of how much they want to

**ROLL CALL:** Rows of Napkin Rolls show variations on a springtime theme of green. Fabric and ribbon "rings" hold rolled napkins in place, while a wide array of buckles, belts, buttons, bows, and other elements gives each roll its own statement, varying from casual to highbrow.

spend, the one area on which I most assuredly don't skimp—without exception—is in the napkin. Your guests will hold it and bring it to their mouths. It stays with them throughout their time at the table. Do you really want to take the cheap and easy route? No one wants a scratchy, nonabsorbent polyester napkin that doesn't do its job or that will leave lint all over their clothes.

Best of all (especially for the budget conscious), a napkin fold costs nothing more than the price of the napkin itself. And it couldn't be easier to do—if you've got the right guide. That's where this book comes in. You're about to discover that whether there are six steps or sixteen, even the most complicated fold is nothing more than a series of simple steps that you can easily master.

*Napkins with a Twist* proffers a bounty of folds—many contemporary adaptations of classic folds, some shown here for the very first time—from which you can choose and which you can make your own.

Going well beyond the basics, there are guidelines for folds so intricate they are literally fit for royalty (see Luigi Spotorno's folds for the House of Windsor, pages 50, 66, and 78). There are classic folds from some of the world's most famous restaurants—Napa Valley's French Laundry, Paris's Restaurant Michel Bras—historic folds drawn from the Kennedy White House and the Clinton White House, and the napkin fold that graced the first-class tables on the ill-fated maiden voyage of the *Titanic*.

You'll also find a wealth of useful tips such as rules of etiquette for setting the table and how to use the napkin fold as a starting point for designing everything from the table itself to the entire event. Whether they enhance a holiday theme, the type of cuisine being served, or a seasonal theme, these are folds that will make it a memorable event for you and your guests.

The napkin folds here follow in the footsteps of centuries of napkin design. Carlyle once remarked that all of history is a distillation of rumor. Some say the napkin concept started with the Spartans, who placed lumps of raw dough on the table so that people could massage them, thus cleansing their fingers. Dough was eventually replaced by more absorbent slices of bread.

However, a critical component in the history of napkins involved the use (or, more to the point, lack of use) of eating utensils. The seemingly barbaric fact that until the early Middle Ages people ate only with their fingers actually promoted the concept of fabrics for wiping fingers and mouths, whether they were tablecloths, table runners, communal towels, or the like.

Ironically, when eating with forks became more popular, napkins fell out of use. Some historians say that the Germanic peoples had such meticulous eating habits that the napkin became pointless. But, by the early fifteenth century, cloth napkins had become increasingly popular in Europe, especially in France and Italy. And then came Louis XIV. Just as the legendary king of France set the tone (and, in some ways, that tone lasts to this day) for throwing a dinner party, he also established the convention of the well-presented dinner napkin as *le must*.

Part of the tabletop legacy included the napkin's fold. During Louis's reign, traces of Asian art and culture began to filter back to the Continent. The art of Japanese paper folding dovetailed perfectly with the desire of royals and aristocrats to embellish the dining table. (And be assured that the tables of Louis XIV were heavily embellished—like a stage set for a spectacle.)

Fast-forward to the present day, when happy-go-lucky party givers and goers have a mission to raise the partying bar. This is our time to make (or change) a little history of our own.

**POCKET CHANGE:** Nothing fancier than a knife and fork is required to fill the Pocket Fold, though the pocket is a great spot to deliver something special to each guest—for example, for a large affair, a program of the evening's events, or perhaps a love note for a two-person affair.

# Some Helpful Guidelines

Unless otherwise specified, all our folds employ large, square dinner napkins (usually 20 inches by 20 inches or larger). Lunch napkins are typically smaller, about 16 inches by 16 inches. Obviously, the smaller the napkin, the more difficult it will be to execute an intricate fold. The same is true of napkins, no matter the size, that are not truly square.

Use napkins made of cotton or linen. Avoid man-made fibers, which can be hard to clean and are often a bit harsh when dabbed across the lips. Even if the guests are lumberjacks, everyone appreciates a gentle touch.

Cheap cloth napkins are rarely a bargain in the long run. They will fray after a few washings and can produce a lot of lint. Is that really fair to a guest dressed in dark blue?

Choose a napkin that matches your table-cloth. In formal settings, white or ivory are the colors of choice. However, colors and patterns are entirely appropriate and work especially well for festive folds such as Shamrock, Tulip, and Party Hat.

When trying out a new fold, practice it a few times to get the hang of it. Once you've mastered the steps, prepare the napkins by pressing them after each step of the fold to set it in place. At first, go slowly to make sure you are getting it right. After the first few, your task will go more quickly.

Except for those folds that require starching to hold their shape, do not use heavy starch on the napkins, either during washing or ironing. Heavy starch cuts down on absorbency—an important function of napkins—and turns a gentle cotton serviette into a stiff square of cloth. If you know that none of your guests is hypoallergenic, as you iron, you can mist each napkin with linen water lightly scented with lavender (see page 45). It will evoke a genuine hint of freshness as the napkin is unfolded.

If you intend to have embroidered text or an image appear on a particular part of your napkin, you need to take a few extra steps. First, make the napkin fold of your choice. Then, using white chalk or an erasable fabric pencil, rough out the area where the stitching or image will go. Unfold the napkin and mark the same area on the other napkins you'll be using. Embroider or apply the image on each napkin. Then, refold the napkin.

Don't present a napkin fold that you haven't been able to conquer. Our designs range from utterly simple to a bit more on the complicated side. It is better to have an exquisitely executed four-fold napkin laid elegantly before your guest than a jumble of wrinkles that looks as if somebody attacked the place setting with an eggbeater.

the folds

# Triple Play

## THE ELEGANT TRIANGLE FOLD

Those who want a fail-safe napkin suitable for an extremely formal occasion need only apply a simple double fold to a white starched square of linen. But since when are you the fail-safe type? You don't go through all the work and love of crafting an elegant soiree to end up with a fold that isn't any different from the twice-folded paper towel you used back in the dorm (though that *was* some awesome pizza!). The Elegant Triangle Fold is not for picnics, business casual, or the timid, but as the name implies, it *is* for the most soigne hosts and elegant occasions. Its muted triangular shape boldly announces formality personified. Its clear-cut shape is so rich, it makes dark blue and burgundy napkins look like evening wear.

**THREE'S A CHARM:** A deep wine Elegant Triangle folded napkin nestled on a lustrous white bone china plate, is a fitting addition to the lush place setting. A toile print tablecloth and etched crystal stemware round out the picture of drop-dead grandeur. The setting is so exquisitely well bred that it easily welcomes the colorful sprigs that grace each plate, as though they were kisses of fun that have fallen from the sky.

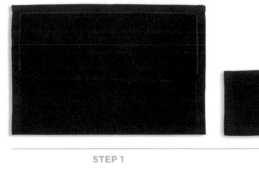

STEP 1                          STEP 2                          STEP 3

STEP 4                          STEP 5                          STEP 6

**1.** Begin with the napkin fully open, laid out as a square, then visually divide the napkin into thirds and fold the bottom third up onto the middle third.

**2.** Fold the top edge down on top of the already folded third so that the top layer completely covers the bottom layer and the edges meet, creating a rectangle. Press.

**3.** Fold the right side of the rectangle over to the left so that the bottom of the rectangle extends 2 inches beyond the top. Press.

**4.** Fold both corners of the top layer of the napkin under to make a point. Press.

**5.** Repeat with the underlayer of the napkin so that you have twin triangular points, the top one about 2 inches smaller than the bottom one. Press.

**6.** Fold the right side of the napkin under a few inches, but no further than where the triangular points begin. Press. Place the napkin so that it points away from the guest.

# ALL IN GOOD TASTE

When you are hosting a formal dinner party, there are lots of ways to be prim that have very little to do with being proper. Snobbery, rigid adherence to the rules of etiquette, and vulgar displays of wealth are turnoffs. Better to serve beer and hot dogs at a table of joyous guests than to suffer through fine cuisine with a room full of stiffs. Still, a little guidance goes a long way toward making everyone feel comfortable. Here are a few pointers to get you started.

## Hosts

• Hand address your invitations. Computer labels are appropriate only for junk mail.

• If you want people to dress up, dress down, or anything in between, state it plainly on the invitation. Hinting won't do.

• Know your guests' food allergies (as in *Are they allergic to meat, fruit, nuts etc.?*) and serve accordingly. If you're not sure, prepare alternative dishes just in case.

• When guests arrive, introduce them to the other guests. Don't leave it to others to handle this most important task: It's your duty.

• Place cards are artful ways of orchestrating the evening's mojo. If guests are hesitant to take their places, it could be because they can't read the cards—don't forget that some people won't be wearing their reading glasses. Offer gentle guidance.

• If guests arrive late, greet them with a warm smile and hearty hello, take their coats, guide them to the table, and say something to make them feel welcome.

• When you've had enough of company, serve coffee. It's the international signal for "get the heck outta here."

## Guests

• An invitation requires an RSVP. Period.

• A dinner party requires that you be on time. End of story.

• Always arrive with a bottle of wine, a box of chocolates, a small gift, or *something*. (Be sure it doesn't have to be used that night.)

• If you're asked to take off your shoes at the door, just do it. It's nothing personal.

• Even if you're not a believer, if the host wants to say grace, go with it.

• If you remember nothing else (we're assuming you know about not talking with your mouth full or chewing with your mouth open—ewww!), don't point—not with your finger, with your hands, or with your knife.

• Turn off your cell phone at the dinner table. If you are truly expecting to be on call for an emergency, turn the phone to vibrate. In the case of that emergency, quietly excuse yourself from the table.

• When you leave, say a gracious, sincere thanks and then get going.

• It is good manners to send a thank-you note. Would it kill you?

# Well Proportioned

## THE THREE-POINT FOLD

For a dashing touch without overdoing it, the Three-Point Fold provides a formal, albeit understated, embellishment to a cultivated place setting. The long, courtly lines are made even more so by using fine white linen given a good once-over with starch and an iron. The design brings to mind the meticulously prim collars found in portraits of dreadfully serious regents by the Dutch masters. Then again, it is also the collar draped around the neck of Frans Hals's *The Merry Drinker.*

**STARCHED, NOT STIFF:** The thoroughly civilized stance of the Three-Point Fold holds its own among the finest, most elaborately decorated settings. Yet the handsome, dignified shape is so quiet that it never competes for attention. True class.

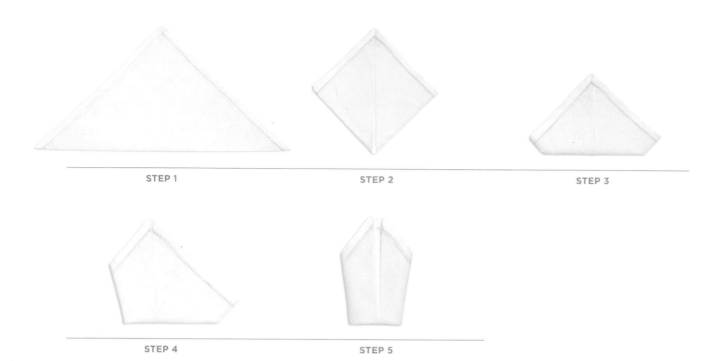

STEP 1                    STEP 2                    STEP 3

STEP 4                    STEP 5

**1.** Begin with the napkin fully open, laid out as a diamond, then fold it in half to create a triangle with the fold at the bottom. Press.

**2.** Fold both the left and right corners to the top point of the triangle, creating a diamond shape with an opening running vertically down the middle. Press.

**3.** Fold under (to the back) just less than half of the lower portion of the diamond. Press.

**4.** Fold under (to the back) the left third of the napkin. Press.

**5.** Repeat the fold on the right third. Press. Place the napkin on the plate with the points at the bottom.

RED WINEGLASS

WHITE WINEGLASS

BUTTER KNIFE

BREAD AND
BUTTER PLATE

DESSERT SPOON •
CAKE FORK

WATER GLASS

DINNER KNIFE

DINNER FORK

FISH KNIFE

SALAD FORK

SOUP-
OR
MELON
SPOON

DINNER PLATE

## PLACES EVERYONE

Though place-setting customs vary from culture to culture, the abiding rule at the dinner table calls for the outermost utensils to be used first. If salad is served first, then the fork farthest left is the salad fork. If fish is served first, then the farthest right knife and farthest left fork are used first. A place setting without a fish fork and knife, for example, means that the meal does not feature a fish course. Similarly, two knives at a meal at which salad is served indicate that one of the knives is for that course. Whether the salad is served before or after the entrée (the latter is the custom in most of Europe) would determine the location of the salad fork and knife, either farther from or closer to the plate.

The side of the plate on which a utensil rests indicates which hand should hold it (though American custom allows for the fork to be shifted from left hand to right after cutting). For formal settings, the dessert fork and spoon are placed at the top of the plate with the handle toward the hand that should use them. Stemware is always to the right, butter dishes always to the left. If you are being served, expect food to come from the left and plates to be removed from the right. Finally, if you or someone at the table makes a gaffe, get over it and enjoy the next course.

# La Isla Bonita

## THE RIPPLE FOLD

George Bernard Shaw once noted that he'd never read a single story about a day in heaven, but he'd read many about a wonderful day at the beach. As inviting as a summer breeze, the Ripple Fold has the seaside air of relaxed pleasure and uncomplicated diversion. The elementary styling of the three overlapping folds (and the purposely chosen aqua-tinged napkin) quietly conjures thoughts of a Windsurfer's sail or, perhaps, a seagull capriciously lolling in an updraft. So easygoing, so happy, no place cards required—but that doesn't mean you can't have them. We've used a child's rubber-stamp set to emblazon the guest's name on a sand dollar. You can almost hear the ocean.

**AM I BLUE?** The cerulean hues of a place setting set in motion by the Ripple Fold rouse thoughts of the ocean. Simple patterns, coloring, and lines click with the tranquil ambience. A sand dollar rubber stamped with each guest's name in blue ink officiates as a place card; strung with twine, it also doubles as a gift— with long twine, it's a necklace; with short twine, a souvenir ornament.

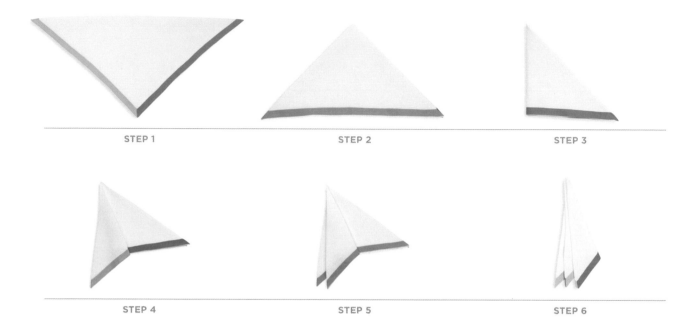

STEP 1          STEP 2          STEP 3

STEP 4          STEP 5          STEP 6

**1.** Begin with the napkin fully open, laid out as a diamond, then fold it once horizontally so that the fold is at the top. Press.

**2.** Fold left to right in half again to make a smaller triangle. Press. Lay out the triangle so that the longest side is at the bottom.

**3.** Fold the napkin in half, laying the left side on top of the right side to make a right triangle.

**4.** To create the fold's narrow, overlapping layers, begin by holding the top point of the triangle down with one hand. With the other hand, grasp the right corner of only the top layer of the napkin and move it until it is pointing at about 7 o'clock.

**5.** Repeat with the second layer, pointing it at 6 o'clock.

**6.** Repeat with the third and final layer, pointing it at about 5 o'clock. Press. *Clambake at sunset!*

# American Beauty

## THE GREENBRIER FOLD

The National Trust for Historic Preservation calls West Virginia's Greenbrier "America's resort," and it isn't difficult to understand why. Founded just two years after the signing of the Declaration of Independence, over the years it has greeted tens of thousands of guests who have found respite in its opulent surroundings, impeccable service, and fine dining. Since its inception, The Greenbrier resort has added golf links, a spa, sporting venues, estate lodging, suites, and eight hundred rooms. Its stately grand dining room, an architectural gem featuring twinkling chandeliers, sets its tables with a reinterpretation of the classic rectangle fold.

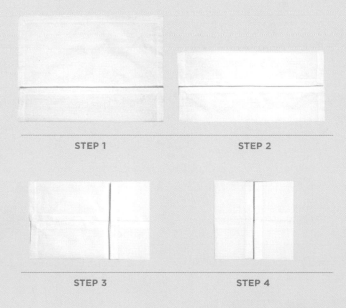

STEP 1          STEP 2

STEP 3          STEP 4

STEP 5

1. Begin with the napkin fully open, laid out as a square, then fold the bottom edge up to the center line of the napkin.

2. Repeat with the upper edge, so that the upper and lower edges meet in the middle. Press.

3. Vertically fold the right edge of the napkin to the center line.

4. Repeat with the left side so that the right and left edges meet in the middle.

5. Fold in half vertically, closing the napkin as though it were a book. Press.

# Garden Variety

## THE SINGLE FLOWER FOLD

This is a fold that takes on any number of personalities, depending on the flower used and the choice of ribbon that ties it all together. For casual affairs, try a sunny daisy plucked from the side of a country road and a gingham ribbon. For a formal wedding, dress up a plush rose or peony by tucking it inside a gossamer organdy ribbon. For anything in between, orchids, sunflowers, zinnias, and black-eyed Susans are among our favorites—not only are they hardy, but they also look good as single blooms. To keep the focus on the flower and ribbon, select a napkin without distracting prints or patterns.

**A BUDDING ROMANCE:** The type of flower and style of ribbon determine the level of formality. Here, a lighthearted setting offers matching tablecloth, napkin, and ribbon in a print that mimics the zinnia. White dinnerware provides a respite from the nearly riotous color. The flowers serve as gifts from the garden for guests to enjoy alongside their place setting, though who could blame them for threading a stem through an open buttonhole or planting their floral garnish to peek out from a breast pocket? To assure freshness, slip the blossom into the tied knot of the ribbon just before guests take their seats.

## WELL SEASONED

Look to the season when you are selecting solitary beauties for your Single Flower Fold.

| | |
|---|---|
| Winter | Calla lilies |
| | French anemones |
| | Gerbera daisies |
| | Holiday foliage & berries |
| | Orchids |
| | Roses |
| Spring | Anemones |
| | Calla lilies |
| | Daffodils |
| | French anemones |
| | Gerbera daisies |
| | Orchids |
| | Peonies |
| | Ranunculi |
| | Roses |
| Summer | Black-eyed Susans |
| | Calla lilies |
| | Daisies |
| | Dahlias |
| | Gerbera daisies |
| | Orchids |
| | Roses |
| | Sunflowers |
| | Zinnias |
| Fall | Calla lilies |
| | Chrysanthemums |
| | Dahlias |
| | Gerbera daisies |
| | Holiday foliage & berries |
| | Orchids |
| | Roses |
| | Sunflowers |
| | Zinnias |

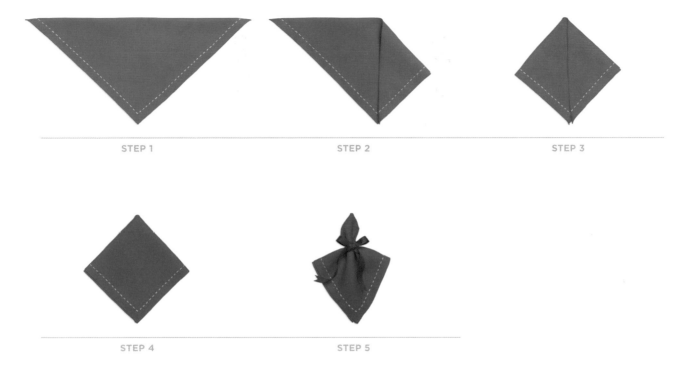

| | |
|---|---|
| STEP 1 | |
| STEP 2 | |
| STEP 3 | |
| STEP 4 | |
| STEP 5 | |

**1.** Begin with the napkin fully open, laid out as a square, then fold the napkin in half horizontally so that the fold is at the top. Press.

**2.** Fold down the right-hand corner of the napkin to meet the center point. Press.

**3.** Repeat with the left-hand corner.

**4.** Flip over the napkin.

**5.** Center a strand of ribbon approximately 15 inches long beneath the upper part of the napkin. Gather the upper part of the napkin together, tying the ribbon around the gathers with a bow. (As in the photograph on page 31, the bottom "tails" of the napkin can be pulled out, if you like.)

Keep flowers in water and, just before guests take their seats, place one bloom in the gathers behind the ribbon.

**ADDITIONAL MATERIALS NEEDED:**
ribbon, fresh flowers

**SAY IT WITHOUT FLOWERS:** The straightforward beauty of the fold is revealed even without a flower. Here, a series of curlicues on a satin ribbon enwraps the gathered folds of a lushly embroidered napkin.

# Message in a Napkin

## THE FORTUNE COOKIE FOLD

Takeout is the last thing most guests expect at a dinner party, but when the cuisine is Chinese, few mind when the order of the day is box after box of fried rice, chow mein, and dishes named after a general. Whether it's takeout or something incredible made in the host's own wok, guests know they're in for a treat when they're greeted by the Fortune Cookie Fold. The sweetest part is the fortune hidden within its folds, but don't forget that what you write has unpredictable implications for the one who receives it. We caution that something as bland as "He who loves you will follow you" could be construed to be an omen to move in with a new boyfriend. By the way, does anybody want that last wonton?

**FENG SHUI:** An oversize fortune peers out from a napkin disguised as a large fortune cookie. What makes the Fortune Cookie Fold successful is how closely the shape and color of the napkin resemble a real fortune cookie. Tiny bits of Chinese calligraphy—all the better if it's accurate—will add to the authenticity of the fortune, but astrological readings, even a love note, will work well, too.

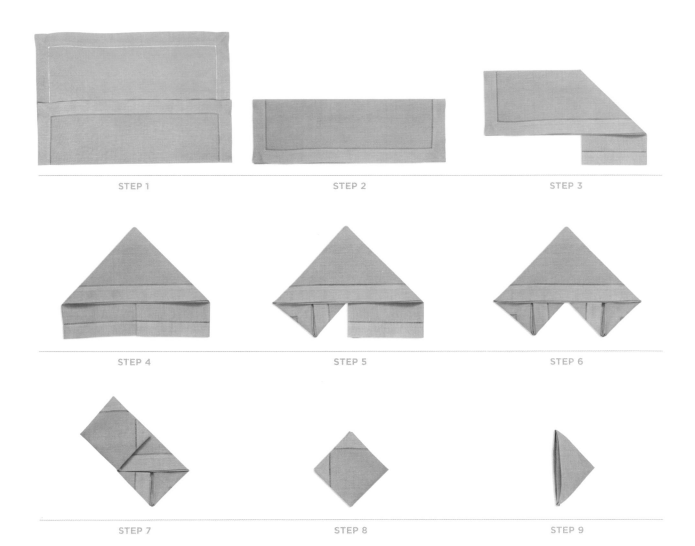

STEP 1     STEP 2     STEP 3

STEP 4     STEP 5     STEP 6

STEP 7     STEP 8     STEP 9

**ADDITIONAL MATERIALS NEEDED:**
paper strips, rubber stamps,
pens, or computer printouts
for fortunes

**NOTE:** Using a golden brown
napkin will help convince your
guests that the napkin looks
like a fortune cookie.

**1.** Begin with the napkin fully open, laid out as a square, then fold the lower edge up one third of the total height of the napkin.

**2.** Fold the top edge down on top of the already folded third so that the top layer completely covers the bottom layer and the edges meet, creating a rectangle. Press.

**3.** With a thumb holding the napkin at the center top edge, fold the right half under itself and pull down so that it extends about 3 inches below the bottom of the rectangle. Press.

**4.** Repeat a mirror-image fold with the upper left half.

**5.** Fold up each of the two corners of the left tail so that they meet at the base of the triangle and form a new triangle with the point at the bottom. Press.

## CHINESE NEW YEAR

For those who aren't quite ready for their annual renewal on January 1, Chinese New Year marks a second chance to set things on course for a fresh start. The holiday is loaded with symbols and significance. For example, don't wear black or white, as these are colors the Chinese associate with mourning. Better to go through your closet and choose something red. The dishes served on Chinese New Year's Eve, the holiday's biggest night, have significance, too, sometimes just because of the Chinese pronunciation of their names. (And, by the way, no fresh tofu. Its whiteness, like white clothes, is associated with misfortune.) Here's a quick rundown of the importance of certain delicacies.

Angel hair seaweed (*fai hai*) = money, prosperity

Shrimp, prawns = exuberance, joy

Raw fish = luck, prosperity

Whole fish = togetherness

Dumplings = make a wish come true

Oysters = goodness

Dried bean curd = wealth, happiness

Bamboo shoots = health

Uncut noodles = long life

Chicken = prosperity

**6.** Repeat with the right tail.

**7.** Holding the right tail in place, grasp the left tail and fold it over to meet the top point.

**8.** In the same way, grasp the outside right point of the right tail and fold it over to meet the top point, creating a diamond shape. Press.

**9.** Fold the diamond in half by bringing the left corner to meet the right corner, making a triangle. Press. Note that the long side of the triangle has a vertical slit where the two folded edges meet.

Open the napkin triangle slightly and prop it up with the vertical-slit opening facing you. Insert the "fortune" into the "cookie."

# Over the Edge

## THE LONG FOLD

In a stark, spare presentation that extends its presence, the Long Fold becomes as integral to the table's adornment as a tablecloth. In fact, the drape—beginning at the center of the place setting and extending to the table's edge and then over the side—is a cascade that's so dramatic and shows so much surface that using several of these napkins on the same table gives the impression of a tablecloth itself. Not that we're trying to take jobs away from any hardworking tablecloth (goodness knows they've earned their place at the table), but napkins bring plenty of fire to the overall mix, especially when they are in colorful patterns, bold lines, and self-confident, voluminous sequencing that lets the napkins speak for themselves.

**DROP CLOTH:** As long as the napkin has even the least bit of pizzazz, it will work with the Long Fold. Keep in mind that in this setting the napkin is eye candy, so other elements of the table setting— tablecloth, dinnerware, and stemware— should be quiet in comparison. And why not? With this fold, the napkin has plenty to say.

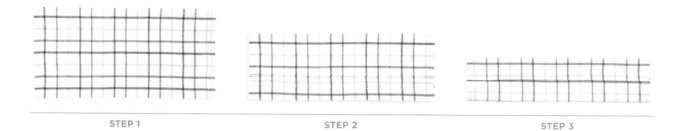

STEP 1 STEP 2 STEP 3

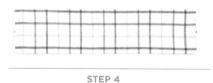

STEP 4

**1.** Begin with the napkin fully open, laid out as a square, then fold the napkin horizontally in half. Press.

**2.** Fold the bottom edge up to meet the middle of the napkin. Press.

**3.** Fold the top edge down to meet the middle of the napkin. Press.

**4.** Flip over the napkin, then rotate it vertically. Drape it over the edge of the table, using a small plate or favorite bowl to keep the napkin in place.

# New York Landmark
## THE PIERRE HOTEL FOLD

*New York* magazine once described The Pierre as a hotel "almost too luxurious for its own good," and anyone who has ever ventured through its canopied Fifth Avenue entrance across from Central Park can understand why. Built in 1929 by hotelier Charles Pierre, it features a grand rotunda with a staggeringly sumptuous trompe l'oeil ceiling and some of the most incredible views of any hotel in the world. Over the years, we've designed many, many events at this sumptuous landmark, including weddings and ceremonies for heads of state, such as President Bill Clinton. Of the various folds employed by The Pierre, this is one of our favorites, and here is our interpretation of it. Like its namesake hotel, the Pierre Fold is a twentieth-century classic.

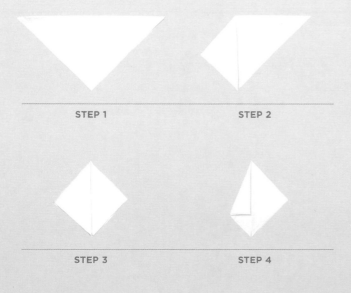

STEP 1    STEP 2

STEP 3    STEP 4

STEP 5    STEP 6

**1.** Begin with the napkin fully open, laid out as a diamond, then fold the top point down to meet the bottom point, creating a triangle with the folded edge at the top. Press.

**2.** Fold the left-hand corner of the triangle down to the bottom point. Press.

**3.** Fold the right-hand corner down to the bottom point, creating a diamond with a vertical slit down the middle.

**4.** Holding the top point down, fold down the left corner to the center so that it meets the vertical slit.

**5.** Repeat in reverse with the right corner. Press.

**6.** Turn the napkin over.

# X Marks the Spot

### THE CRISSCROSS FOLD

At an increasing number of occasions—not just weddings, but teas, baby and bridal showers, and other events—guests find small gifts waiting for them at their place setting. Rather than have the gift and the napkin compete for space, the Crisscross Fold melds the two functions of napkin and gift holder while also playing an integral part in the table decor. The conspicuously sharp lines of the fold, made especially pronounced in starched white linen, create an impeccable launch pad for a little gift, toy, or, perhaps, a most intriguing *amuse-bouche*—a single, exquisite chocolate preciously wrapped and tied.

**GIFTED:** An impossibly beautiful napkin edged in a diaphanous trim of airy crocheted lace is sublimely showcased with the Crisscross Fold. The beauty is intensified by adding a tiny gift almost too pretty to open but too gorgeous not to. What's inside, though, is beside the point. A bright cabochon illuminates the jeweled nature of the gift itself and its importance to the decor. The ribbon, gift wrap, and tablecloth interplay in an ombré of deep purple that fades to dusty lavenders.

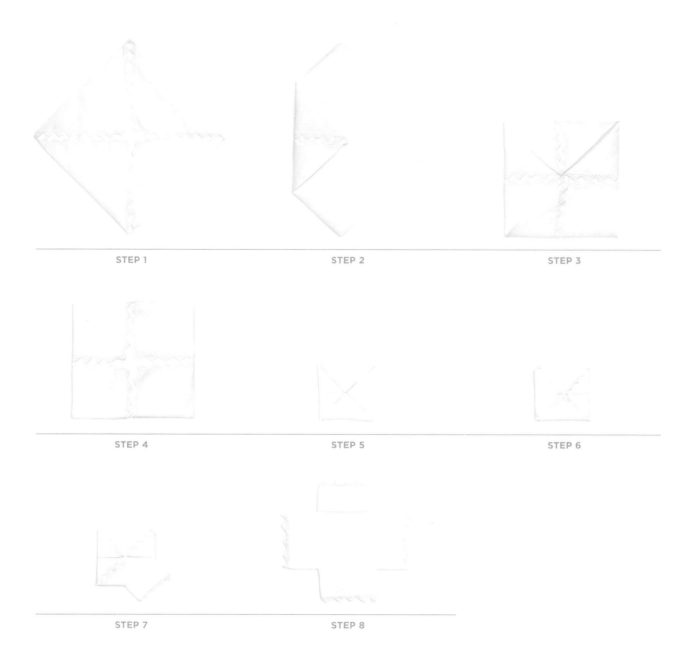

STEP 1

STEP 2

STEP 3

STEP 4

STEP 5

STEP 6

STEP 7

STEP 8

**1.** Begin with the napkin fully open, laid out as a square, then fold each corner to the center, creating a diamond. Press.

**2.** Flip the napkin over. Fold the left corner to the center line.

**3.** Fold the remaining corners to the center line as in step 1.

**4.** With one hand holding the four points in place and the other hand completely underneath the square that was formed, flip the square over, being careful to keep the shape.

## A SIMPLE RECIPE FOR HOMEMADE LINEN WATER
### Lavender Linen Water

A well-laced spritz of linen water adds a wonderful fragrance and smoothness, especially when judiciously applied to napkins just before ironing. We asked Eric Loos of San Francisco's Nancy Boy, maker of botanical products for the bath, body, and home (www.nancyboy.com), for an easy way to create your own linen water at home. His recipe follows:

2 ounces of the highest proof vodka available

¾ ounce lavender essential oil

14 ounces distilled water
(slightly less than a pint)

16-ounce clear plastic or glass spray bottle

In a small glass bowl, stir the vodka and essential oil together until thoroughly mixed. Pour distilled water into the spray bottle and add the vodka-oil mixture. Shake gently. The mixture may cloud, but this is normal, and the formula will not stain clothes or laundry. To keep ingredients well mixed, gently shake the bottle before each use.

**5.** Fold each corner to the center line once again.

**6.** Flip the napkin over

**7.** The napkin now has four quadrants, each with a diagonal opening. Gently pull the center point of the lower right quadrant toward the outer edge of the napkin to make the first of the rectangular legs of the crisscross.

**8.** Repeat with the remaining three quadrants. Press. At each place setting, position the napkin as either an X or a plus (+) sign.

# Be a Clown

**THE PARTY HAT FOLD**

Despite admonitions to the contrary, sometimes clowning around is entirely appropriate at the table. When the occasion calls for a particularly festive setting, this napkin trumpets that it's time to party. Spectacularly boisterous patterns work well here, and can then be played out throughout the rest of the table—even the food (imagine cupcakes speckled with candy confetti or tiny tarts adorned with goofy faces dribbled in raspberry sauce). This napkin is especially suited for birthdays and all fashion of celebratory lunches and dinners where the mood is so bubbly that only a party hat can keep a lid on the excitement.

**THE POINT IS MADE:** No fabric pattern is too outlandish for this fold. And by choosing a wild napkin print, you'll have plenty of options for completing the event's decorating scheme. We've adorned this party hat with a fluffy pom-pom, but other trinkets would also work. A tiny bell, for example, would add a happy tinkling jingle to the affair.

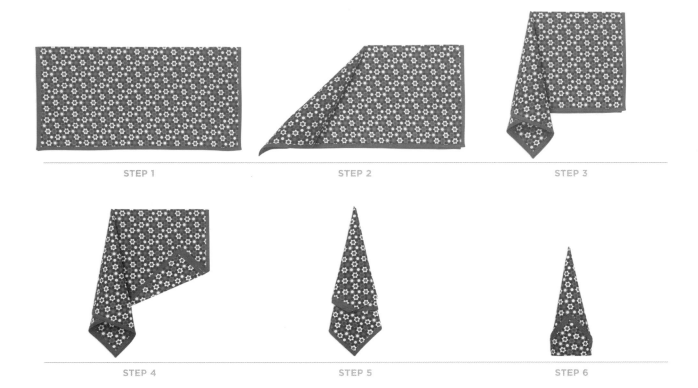

STEP 1    STEP 2    STEP 3

STEP 4    STEP 5    STEP 6

**ADDITIONAL MATERIALS NEEDED:**
pom-poms, thread to match the color of the pom-poms, sewing needle, scissors

1. Begin with the napkin fully open, laid out as a square, then fold it in half horizontally so that the fold is at the top. Press.

2. With one finger of your right hand, hold the center of the top fold of the napkin. With your left hand, loosely roll down the left-hand corner, working toward a cone shape.

3. Continue rolling the cone toward the center of the napkin, stopping the roll when the point, or tail, is centered at the back of the cone.

4. With one finger of your left hand holding the napkin down at the bottom of the center crease, grasp of the lower right corner with your right hand and fold up about 2 inches toward the top of the napkin. Press.

5. Roll the cone completely and tuck in the loose point in between the layers of the cone.

**6.** Flip over the napkin so that the front of the cone faces you. Fold the tail of the cone up to create a "cuff" that is 3 or 4 inches high in the front. Press.

With thread and a needle, sew a tiny, festive pom-pom at the top (point) of the hat. *Party on.*

**SEND IN THE CLOWNS:** An array of party hat napkins stands ready for duty. The print pattern of the napkins is reflected in the button-size candy speckles on the cupcakes, as well as on the tablecloth, which is embroidered with tiny stitched dots. The setting is buffet style so that when each guest takes a napkin, it comes complete with the necessary utensils—in this case, plastic forks doing double duty as feathers in a cap.

# Sitting Pretty
## THE THRONE FOLD*

Fifty years after Elizabeth II became Queen of England, Great Britain officially launched Golden Jubilee celebrations in her honor. Not *a* celebration, mind you, *celebrations*. From May to August 2002, the Queen and the Duke of Edinburgh traveled almost nonstop throughout England, Scotland, and Wales to festivities being held in their honor. Elizabeth even granted her subjects an extra bank holiday. To commemorate the Golden Jubilee, Luigi Spotorno created the Throne Fold as well as the Coronation Fold (see page 78). Though these designs may be a bit too dazzling for most, they may come in handy should the guest of honor be, at the very least, "Queen for a Dinner."

**NOTE:** Napkins must be heavily starched, and the folds pressed frequently.

1. Begin with the starched napkin fully open, laid out as a square, then fold it in half horizontally so that the folded edge is at the bottom. Press.

2. Fold the upper right corner down diagonally so that the corner meets the bottom edge at the center of the napkin. Press.

3. Fold the napkin's right side down to the left to create an even 4-inch band.

4. Flip the napkin over so that the longest side is at the bottom.

5. Fold the bottom edge of the napkin up so that it folds the band in half. Press.

6. Flip the napkin over, keeping the longest side at the bottom.

7. Fold the left end to the right so that the point lies directly below the top point of the triangle.

8. Fold the far right corner of the napkin to the left, folding the triangle in half and creating another triangle. Press.

9. Tuck the left point and top layer of the now-folded triangle into the folds of the band.

10. At the bottom, open the folded triangle to create a circle, forming the base of the crown, and stand the napkin upright. At the table, place the point of the crown toward the back (pointing away from the guest).

*Created to celebrate the Golden Jubilee of HM Queen Elizabeth II (1952–2002)

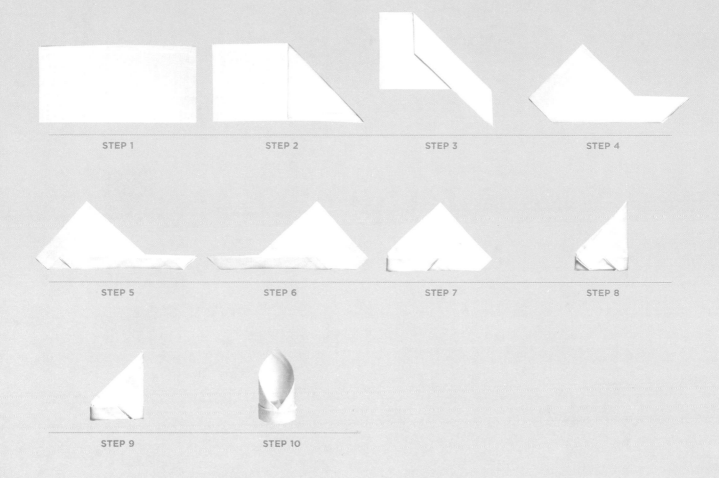

STEP 1 STEP 2 STEP 3 STEP 4

STEP 5 STEP 6 STEP 7 STEP 8

STEP 9 STEP 10

## LUIGI SPOTORNO, ROYAL FOLDER

"Fit for a queen" is a phrase taken quite seriously at Buckingham Palace. From cheese and chocolates to pork sausage and whiskey, goods supplied to the royal family must pass the strictest standards of quality. Those who achieve royal recognition can then proudly boast of being "Purveyors to Her Majesty the Queen" on their labels. Luigi Spotorno doesn't have a label, but he does have a knack for whipping up linen creations that make their way onto royal tables. A native of Italy, Spotorno has served as a dining steward on luxury ocean liners, as a restaurant manager at several fine hotels in Great Britain, and as a banquet and hospitality manager. Besides the Throne, the Prince of Wales, and Coronation folds included in this book (see also pages 66 and 78), he also created the Royal Crest Fold in honor of the 1999 wedding of Prince Edward, Elizabeth's youngest child, and Wings of Hope, a fold to celebrate the new millennium. He is currently working on his own book of folds.

# In Clover

## THE SHAMROCK FOLD

You don't have to be Irish to enjoy this fold (remember even Saint Patrick wasn't Irish), just lucky enough to be seated at a table with good friends, family, food, and drink. Though your guests might dine on a traditional meal of corned beef and cabbage, the stiff peaks of the fold are equally at home at a fancy feast (one perhaps finished with an Irish apple and barley pudding). Obviously, a solid green napkin is an ideal choice, but variations, such as a bright green plaid, would be fun, too. Curved stems can be added to serve as a place card. A table festooned with these four-leaf clovers signals an occasion filled with mirth and warmth. If the evening just happens to fall on March 17, well then, *begorra!,* all the better!

**LUCKY YOU:** The well-groomed lines of the Shamrock Fold mean it can serve in most dressy affairs, while the easy charm of the symbol makes it also fitting for casual doings. A box of tiny clovers dressed up in green reiterates the theme. Eyelets in the tablecloth allow a glimpse of the green table cover beneath.

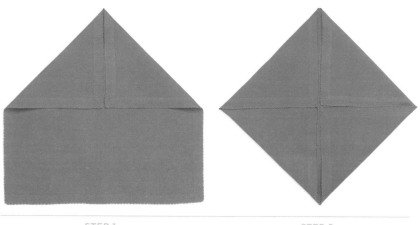

**NOTE:** This fold works best with a nicely starched napkin.

1. Begin with the napkin fully open, laid out as a square, then fold the two upper corners in to meet in the middle.

2. Repeat with the lower two corners to make a diamond. Press.

3. Bring each point of the diamond to the center line so that the four points meet in the middle and make a square. Press.

4. With one hand holding the four points in place and the other hand completely underneath the square, flip the entire square over, being careful to keep the shape.

5. Bring each corner of the napkin to the center again. After all four corners are brought to the center, press, and then position the napkin as a square.

6. While holding down the center intersection of the four points with one hand, with the other hand, reach behind each corner and partially unfold the fabric beneath so that each corner now has two layers. Gently pull the point of each corner's lower layer just until the upper layer peaks up.

**7.** Fold the lower layer under each corner about 1 inch toward the napkin's center. Gently pull the upper layers' folds open toward the four corners while being sure to keep all the center folds in place. Steam lightly. *You're looking over your four-leaf clover!*

**GREEN GARNISH:** A decorative fabric cut in the shape of a shamrock stem and embroidered with a guest's name in contrasting thread snuggles within the folds. An easier and entirely satisfying alternative is to make the stem from construction paper and embellish it with a marker.

# Ship Shape

## THE SAILBOAT FOLD

You don't have to be seaside to make a splash at your next dinner party. Even an event in the middle of the desert will find an oasis in this nautical theme. The right menu, some cool libations, and a few visual cues alert guests that the course has been set for a lively dining adventure (sea shanties optional). Though not a must, a napkin with a contrasting edge trim will give your "boat" a jaunty racing stripe. With their own personal sailboat to catch the fun, young and young-at-heart diners set sail at spring and summertime affairs.

**AHOY:** Blues and nautical themes abound with a pot of dark blue hydrangeas wrapped in bright white sailor's twine, trimmed in, yes, blue. It's a setting that will find a friendly port even with the most ardent landlubber. The captain, first mate, and crew are ready to embark on their pleasure cruise.

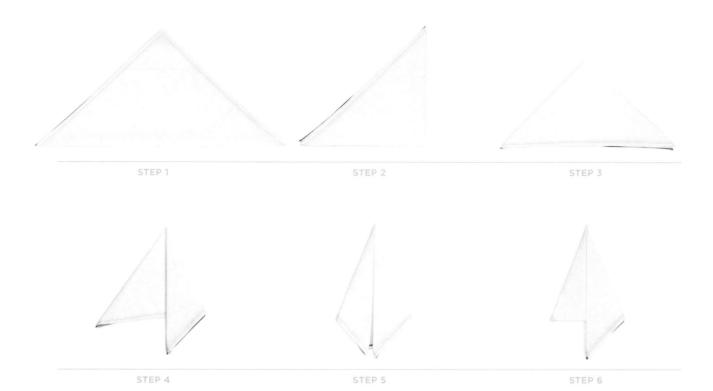

STEP 1

STEP 2

STEP 3

STEP 4

STEP 5

STEP 6

**1.** Begin with the napkin fully open, laid out as a diamond, with the trimmed side up, then fold it in half to make a triangle with the fold at the bottom. Press.

**2.** Fold it in half again, right corner to left, to make a right triangle. Press.

**3.** Rotate the napkin so that the long side of the triangle is at the bottom.

**4.** Fold the right corner toward the center of the napkin so that the right side of the triangle now forms a vertical line down the middle, the lower point extending below the bottom of the triangle.

**5.** Repeat with the left corner so that the two sides now meet in the center. Press.

**6.** Fold the left corner that extends below the triangle up under itself until it is flush with the bottom of the triangle and tuck it behind the first layer.

**7.** Repeat with the right side to make a compact triangle. Press.

**8.** Carefully roll up the bottom edge to make a "cuff" around the front and back of the triangle. (Be sure to roll the layer with the trimmed edge.)

**9.** When you are finished, crease the bottom with your finger. A once-over with an iron will keep the shape, and a bit of starch will allow you even to stand the boat upright. *Set sail!*

**SHE'S A GRAND (IF TINY) FLAG:** Paper pennants outlined in blue match the napkin trim and serve as place cards. We've printed our guest's name in blue on a computer, but a marker works fine, too. The place card pennants are glued around one end of a toothpick that's then tucked into the tip-top of the upright vessel.

# Opulence and Arrogance
## THE *TITANIC* FOLD

Hundreds of important seagoing vessels were lost in the early part of the twentieth century, yet it is the sinking of the *Titanic* on her maiden voyage from Southampton, England, to New York in 1912 that remains galvanized in the public's memory. Perhaps it was the extraordinary wealth of many of the ship's first-class passengers, who included Astors and Guggenheims, and the dazzling opulence in which they traveled (the *Titanic* Fold, with its dense intricacy, hints at the decadence). It's more likely, however, that the folly of the ship's promoters—who claimed that the *Titanic* was "practically unsinkable" and put far too few lifeboats aboard to serve the ship's two thousand passengers, of whom more than fifteen hundred died—is what casts the ill-fated story as a cautionary tale of the price of hubris.

### DECADENCE IN TEN COURSES

The cuisine served aboard the *Titanic* varied according to the class of passenger. Not surprisingly, first-class passengers enjoyed an over-the-top dinner menu that ran a full ten courses, not counting the fruit and cheese plates served at the end. Each course was accompanied by its own wine, and after dessert, postprandial snifters of port and cigars were served to the gentlemen. Typical menu items included oysters, consommé Olga (made with the spinal marrow of sturgeon), paupiette of salmon with scallop mousseline, filet mignon in a Perigord foie gras sauce, chicken lyonnaise, roast duckling, beef sirloin, lamb, roast squab, rice, creamed carrots, peas, potatoes Parmentier and potatoes Anna, plover eggs, applesauce, asparagus vinaigrette, pâté, and, for dessert, peaches in chartreuse jelly, chocolate and vanilla éclairs, Waldorf pudding, and French ice cream.

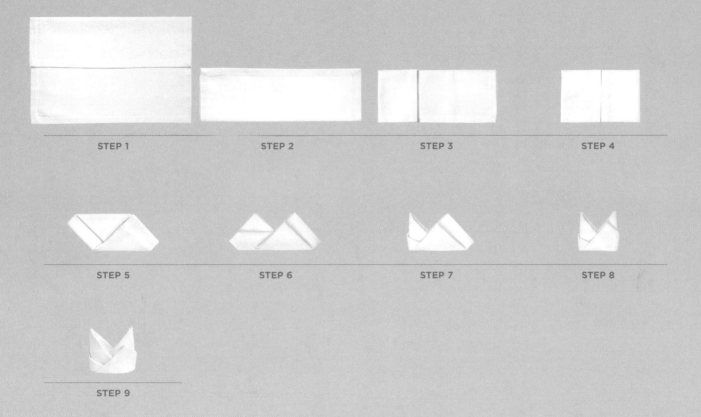

STEP 1 | STEP 2 | STEP 3 | STEP 4

STEP 5 | STEP 6 | STEP 7 | STEP 8

STEP 9

**NOTE:** This fold works best with a napkin that has a nicely starched finish.

1. Begin with the napkin fully open, laid out as a square, then fold the upper edge down one third of the total height of the napkin.

2. Fold the bottom edge up horizontally on top of the already folded third so that the top layer completely covers the bottom layer and the edges meet, creating a rectangle. Press.

3. Fold the left-hand side of the rectangle to the center line. Press.

4. Fold the right-hand side of the rectangle to the center line. Press.

5. Fold the upper left corner down and the lower right corner up to make two right triangles whose sides meet but leave about 2 inches of the rectangle exposed on each side. Rotate the

napkin clockwise so that the center line is at a diagonal. Press.

6. This part is a little tricky, so take your time. Grasp both triangles at their centers, one in each hand. Pick up the napkin and, with your thumbs placed on the center of each triangle, fold the left side back, keeping the points of the triangles up. Lay the napkin down on the table so that the two "peaks" face up. Press.

7. Grasp the left side of the left peak and fold it in half toward the center, tucking the end into the folds of the uppermost triangle on the right side.

8. Flip the entire napkin over and repeat step 7, folding the left side of the left peak in half and then tucking the end into the folds of the uppermost triangle on the right side.

9. Stand the napkin upright at the place setting.

# To the Letter

## THE MONOGRAM FOLD

While Shakespeare pondered "What's in a name?" we've been considering "What's in a monogram?" Perhaps the answer lies in the Monogram Fold, a napkin that showcases the embroidered beauty of capital Helvetica letters, lowercased italics, Gothic initials, and other sorts of stitched lettering. During modern times, monograms have experienced varying degrees of popularity, ranging from the ridiculousness of "his and hers" towels, which bordered on parody, to the subdued charm of a single raised letter sewn in thread color-matched to the host fabric. On napkins, monograms—typically the first initial of the hosts' last name—harken back to centuries of tradition in embroidered or needlepoint samplers. A crisp circle of stitched dots around a solitary letter updates it with a hip twist.

**LETTER PERFECT:** Monogrammed napkins are a tasteful statement, even when stitched in the subtle fashion shown here. The Monogram Fold would look good without any needlework, but it provides a worthy platform when fine handiwork deserves to be discretely flaunted. The embroidered circle around the letter nicely mimes the dots that border the plate and the embroidered dots of the table linen.

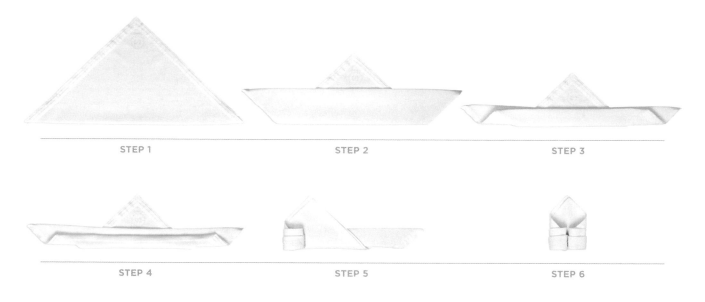

STEP 1     STEP 2     STEP 3

STEP 4     STEP 5     STEP 6

STEP 7

**NOTE:** This fold requires a napkin that already has been monogrammed on one corner.

**1.** Begin with the napkin fully open, laid out as a diamond, with the monogram face down and positioned at the bottom. Fold the bottom point up to the top point, making a triangle with the folded edge at the bottom. Press.

**2.** Fold the bottom edge up horizontally to the top, leaving the peak of the triangle and the monogram uncovered.

**3.** Fold the horizontal band in half by bringing the bottom edge up to meet the top edge of the fold.

**4.** Fold down the top layer, creating a 1-inch-wide band at the center, and hold the three parts in place. Press.

**5.** Flip the entire napkin over so that the triangle's point is at the top. Roll the left side in to rest at the center.

**6.** Repeat with the right side so that *both* sides meet at the center. Press.

**7.** Flip the napkin over and position it at the place setting so that the monogram properly faces the guest.

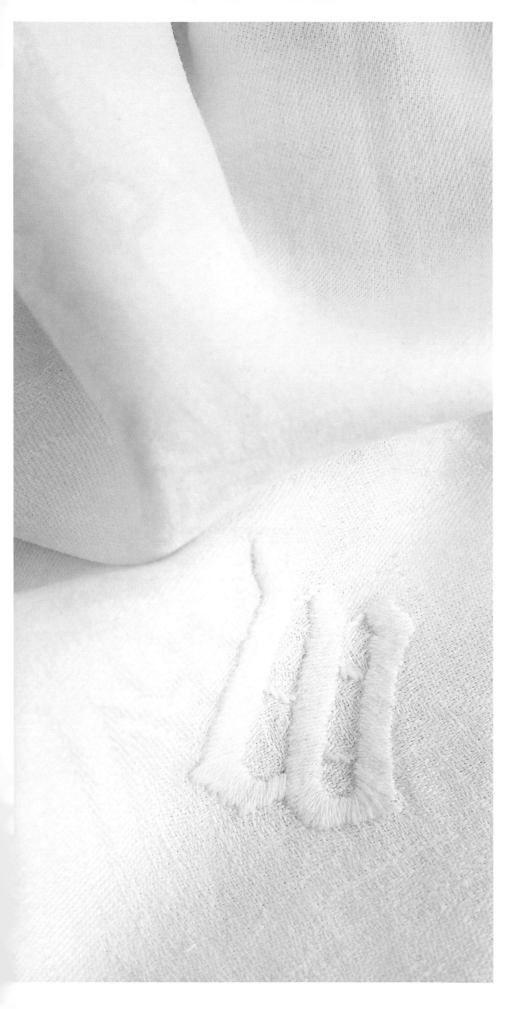

**CAPITAL IDEA:** A classic three-initial monogram in a serif font is a richly textured addition to the napkin. When embroidering a monogram of three initials, the last-name initial is placed in the center and is larger than the other two letters. The first initial is placed to the left and the middle initial to the right of the last-name initial, as in GSB for George Bernard Shaw.

**INITIAL RESPONSE:** A single letter in Old English script, sewn in linen thread that matches the color of the linen napkin, exhibits quiet good taste that you can see and feel.

# Charles in Charge
## THE PRINCE OF WALES FOLD*

The long-simmering love between Charles, Prince of Wales, and Camilla Parker Bowles was perhaps England's worst-kept secret. After having met in the early 1970s, Charles and Camilla were smitten, but their love would have to wait until the end of a proper mourning period after the death of Princess Diana. Finally, nearly three decades after their first encounter, they were married in a civil ceremony in 2005. To honor the occasion, Luigi Spotorno crafted the Prince of Wales Fold, a design that is intricate in its layers and tucks, yet thoroughly modern, with an irregular, natural silhouette.

**NOTE:** The napkin *must* be heavily starched.

1. Begin with the napkin fully open, laid out as a diamond, then horizontally fold the bottom point up to about 4 inches from the top point and directly below it. Press.

2. Flip the napkin over so that the folded edge is at the bottom.

3. Quickly fold the napkin in half and unfold it to create a slight center line. With one finger holding the center of the bottom folded edge, fold the lower left corner of the napkin up about 2 inches to create a slim, long triangle.

4. Repeat in reverse on the right side. Press.

5. With one finger again holding the center of the bottom folded edge, fold the right side of the napkin up so that it meets an imaginary center line, leaving the top point resting approximately 2 inches below the bottom point.

6. Repeat in reverse on the right. Press.

7. Starting at the bottom, horizontally fold up the bottom point twice, making a 2-inch-wide band at the base.

8. Fold the band up over itself two more times. Press.

9. Flip the entire napkin over, being careful to keep all the folds in place.

*Created for and used at the wedding of Prince Charles to Camilla Parker Bowles.

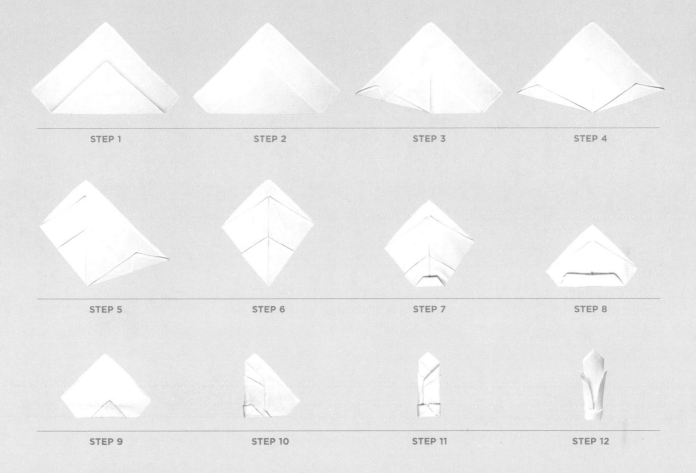

STEP 1  STEP 2  STEP 3  STEP 4

STEP 5  STEP 6  STEP 7  STEP 8

STEP 9  STEP 10  STEP 11  STEP 12

**10.** Vertically fold the left corner of the napkin twice to the right, resting it just past the center vertical line.

**11.** Repeat step 10 in reverse, bringing the right corner over almost completely to the left edge. Press. Tuck the base of the right-side fold into the band of the lower left side.

**12.** Turn the napkin over, open the base (the band) into a small circle, and set the napkin upright. At the place setting, separate the twin front points of the napkin to resemble an iris.

# Fit to Be Untied

## THE SQUARE GIFT FOLD

A German proverb says that a small gift is better than a great promise. This is a fold with both. Its dainty pleats, crowned with a double-leaf bow, promise guests that something wonderful awaits. The fold is intended to wrap a small, but not too small, cubelike box. A box slightly narrower than a credit card should work. What you put in it should reflect your own tastes and offer a connection between guest and host. It may contain a simple token of affection—a charm bracelet for a Sweet 16 party, a tiny framed photo for a family gathering—or something more intimate, such as a piece of fine jewelry. This is not, however, the time for gag gifts (such as condoms at a baby shower) and nothing mundane (candy, a golf ball and tee, a candle). The presentation is too substantial to let the wrapping promise more than it delivers.

**NOTE:** The napkin must be heavily starched.

1. Begin with a well-starched napkin fully open, laid out as a square, then make a 1-inch-deep pleat at the center of the napkin. Press.

2. In the same way, create a second 1-inch-deep pleat beneath, parallel, and on the top of the first pleat so that it's about $\frac{1}{2}$ inch from the folded edge of the first pleat. Press.

3. As in step 2, make a third pleat 1 inch from the second. Press.

4. Carefully turn the napkin over so that it is laid out as a diamond.

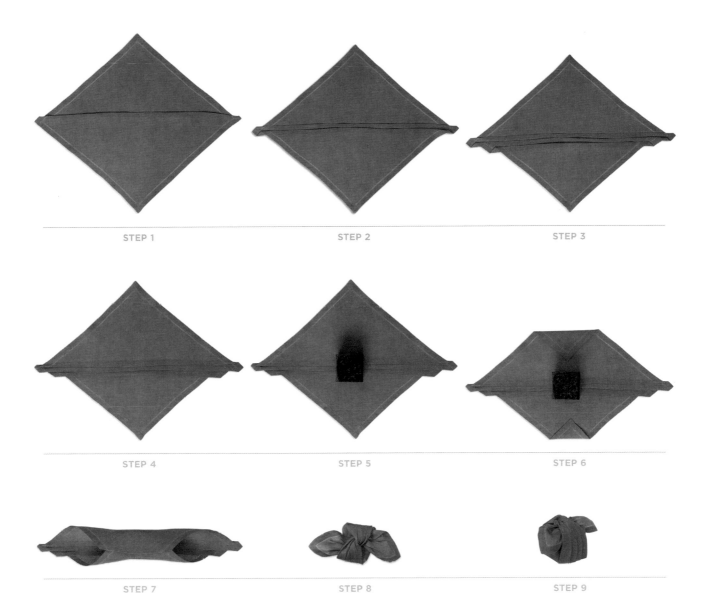

STEP 1      STEP 2      STEP 3

STEP 4      STEP 5      STEP 6

STEP 7      STEP 8      STEP 9

**5.** Place a small square gift box in the center of the napkin (and don't forget to include a gift inside!).

**6.** Fold the corners in toward the gift box to create straight edges.

**7.** Fold these straight-edged sides up and over the gift, having both flat edges meet at the top of the box.

**8.** Bring the left and right sides of the napkin up to the top of the box and carefully knot the two ends so that the pleats stay in place.

**9.** Curl under the outer edges of the knotted ends so that they look like two leaves. *That's a wrap.*

# Your Name Here

## THE PLACE CARD FOLD

Place cards aren't just for assigning seats. The strategic placement of each invitee can diplomatically split clinging couples, give glib gabbers a ready audience, and *make* wallflowers blossom. Enlisting the Place Card Fold to present seat assignments makes the most of a table's valuable real estate. Besides as name plates, the assured rolls of the fold can be trusted to prop up other choice bits of ephemera, from baby pictures of the man of honor to postcards that celebrate the reunion of friends from a college semester in Dakar (would you believe a great weekend in Cleveland?).

**IS THIS SEAT TAKEN?** The trim lines of the Place Card Fold frame the all-important information that will guide all guests to just the right spot and ensure they will enjoy a most agreeable affair. The yellow and cornflower blue of the napkin reverberate throughout the setting, including the sunflower theme of the tablecloth, centerpiece, and place card. Places everyone!

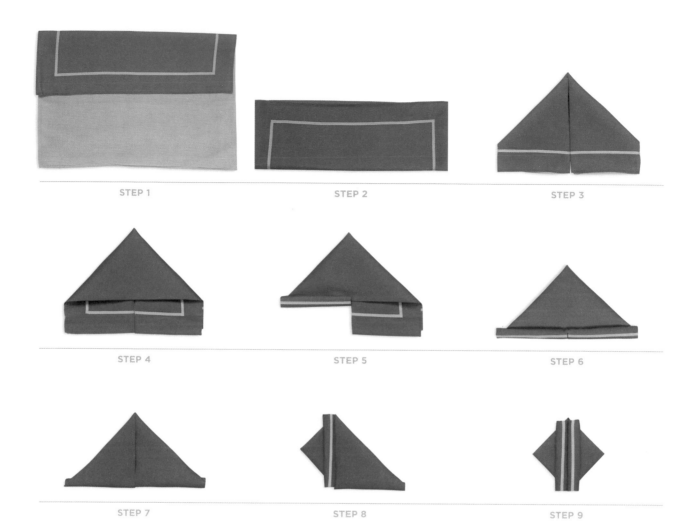

**1.** Begin with the napkin fully open, laid out as a square, then fold the top edge down one third of the total height of the napkin. Press.

**2.** Fold the bottom edge up on top of the already folded third so that the top layer completely covers the bottom layers and the edges meet.

**3.** Fold the napkin in half and then unfold, leaving a center vertical line to work from. With the imaginary vertical center line, fold each top corner down so that they meet at the center line.

**4.** Flip over the napkin with the point at the top. You now have a triangle on top with two "tails" that extend beneath its bottom edge.

## PLACE CARDS AND THEIR PLACE

Place cards serve a number of purposes. The most important is that creative seating arrangements can enliven a table. They spare guests the need to decide where—and with whom—to sit. That breaks up cliques and makes solo fliers feel welcome. Finally, place cards free the host from arranging the table as the meal is beginning. A few points of note:

- Seat guests of honor to the right of the host or, at a round table, across from the host.

- At weddings, the groom sits to the right of the bride. For the wedding party, you have two options: Seat the maid of honor to the groom's right and the best man to the bride's left, or seat the best man next to the groom and the maid of honor next to the bride.

- When there's only one table, the hosts sit at opposite ends of the table except when there is a guest of honor, who then sits opposite one host and next to the other.

- Use Mr. and Ms. with surnames (formal), first and last names (less formal), or first names only (informal), but be consistent.

- At large gatherings, couples and close friends commonly sit at the same table, but not necessarily next to one another. (The exception is engaged couples, who are seated next to each other.) It's OK to split up groups, but make sure that each person at a table knows at least one other person. It's cool to pair singles, but don't put them all at the same table.

- At large gatherings, place the younger set near the band or speakers (crazy kids!) and family members near the head table.

- A guest who rearranges place cards without permission can expect to be eighty-sixed from all future events.

**5.** Roll up the left tail onto the triangle.

**6.** Roll up the right tail onto the triangle. You may need to hold the first roll in place as you roll the second.

**7.** Holding the rolls in place, flip the napkin over.

**8.** Fold the bottom-left rolled edge up to meet the center line.

**9.** Fold the bottom-right rolled edge up to meet the left. Slide your place card between them. *Please be seated.*

# To the Nines

### THE TUXEDO FOLD

All dressed up and somewhere to go. Just as tastemakers have anointed the tuxedo as de rigueur for occasions that unflinchingly celebrate the good life, the opulent and chichi Tuxedo Fold dresses up the most luxurious tables. This grand creation is extremely easy to construct and not so rococo that it will upstage the place setting or the table. There's even a pocket cut on the bias, a perfect place to spotlight the evening's menu. Rather rakish, no?

**PUTTING ON THE RITZ:** The exactingly elegant Tuxedo Fold is formal wear for the table, a debonair theme played out in the pleated tablecloth and the square flower box studded with black buttons. A handwritten menu adorned with a natty, black bow tie in miniature is cut to the same width as the finished napkin and inserted behind the top roll.

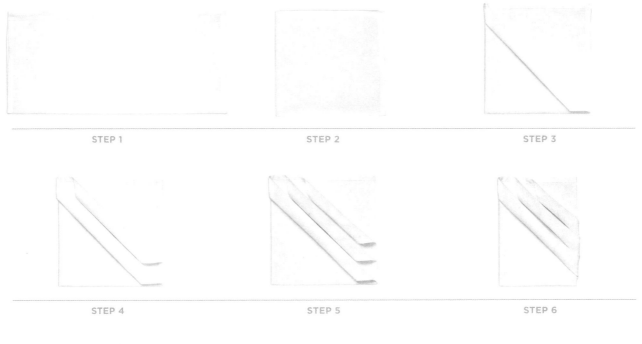

STEP 1          STEP 2          STEP 3

STEP 4          STEP 5          STEP 6

STEP 7

**ADDITIONAL MATERIALS NEEDED:**
miniature bow ties

**1.** Begin with the napkin fully open, laid out as a square, then fold the napkin in half horizontally, with the folded edge at the bottom. Press.

**2.** Vertically fold the napkin in half again to make a square, with the folded edges at the left and bottom. Press.

**3.** Beginning with the upper right corner of the top layer of the napkin, roll the corner toward the center—for example, as though you were making a roll of dimes—until the roll extends from the upper left corner to the lower right corner but does not extend outside of the square. Press.

**4.** Repeat step 3 with the second layer of the napkin, beginning at the upper right corner and rolling until you meet the first roll.

**5.** Repeat step 3 with the third layer of the napkin. You should now have three even diagonal rolls lying side by side. Press.

**6.** Beginning at the lower right corner (where the rolls end), vertically fold one third the width of the napkin to the back in order to hold the rolls in place.

**7.** Beginning at the upper left corner (where the rolls begin), repeat step 6. Press. *A true classic.*

## A MAN'S WEAR-WITH-ALL

When the invitation specifically lists expected attire, dress accordingly. While women have some latitude in what to wear, men's guidelines are fairly specific. To wit:

| If the invitation says . . . | Then wear . . . |
| --- | --- |
| Black tie | Tuxedo |
| Black tie optional | Tuxedo or dark suit |
| White tie | Black or white tailcoat, black pants, white shirt, tie, and vest (remember to leave the bottom button of the vest unbuttoned) |
| Casual evening attire | Shirt and slacks, jacket optional |
| Informal evening attire | Jacket and tie |
| Formal evening attire | *See* Black tie |
| Jacket required | Oh, come now! |
| Business casual | Anything from khakis to sport coats—check with your hosts |
| Casual | Comfortable clothes (jeans are fine)—avoid tank tops, sleeveless T-shirts, and cutoffs |
| Resort casual | A cut above casual |
| Dressy resort casual | Button-down or polo shirt, slacks, shoes or sandals, nice shorts (daytime only), sport coat optional |
| Festive | Have some fun! (Did we *really* have to tell you that?) |

# Crowning Achievement
## THE CORONATION FOLD*

In 1953, twenty-seven-year-old Elizabeth Alexandra Mary of the House of Windsor was crowned Queen Elizabeth II, the titular head of state for Great Britain and the Commonwealth. Even her coronation was an early indication of her independence from royal traditions; it was the first coronation to be broadcast on live television to her twenty million subjects and other people around the world. The governing cabinet ministers, including Winston Churchill, had previously rejected television coverage inside Westminster Abbey (for fear the lights and cameras would prove too much of a distraction for her), but Elizabeth would have none of it. "The cabinet's not being crowned," she told Churchill. "I am." And so she was. For much of the ceremony, Elizabeth sat on a magnificent oak throne carved for King Edward I in 1300. For the Golden Jubilee of Elizabeth's rule, Luigi Spotorno used the Coronation Chair, and its achingly high-pointed back, for inspiration for The Coronation Fold napkin.

**NOTE:** Napkins must be heavily starched, and folds pressed frequently.

1. Begin with a starched napkin fully open, laid out as a square, then fold it in half horizontally so that the folded edge is at the bottom. Press.

2. Diagonally fold down both layers of the upper right corner to the center of the napkin's edge, creating a triangle on the right side of the napkin. Press the folded diagonal edge.

3. Create a 1-inch pleat along the diagonal edge of the triangle as follows: Grasp the top layer of the triangle and, keeping the folded diagonal edge in place, fold the corner up and to the right.

*Created to celebrate the fiftieth anniversary of the Queen's Coronation (1953–2003)

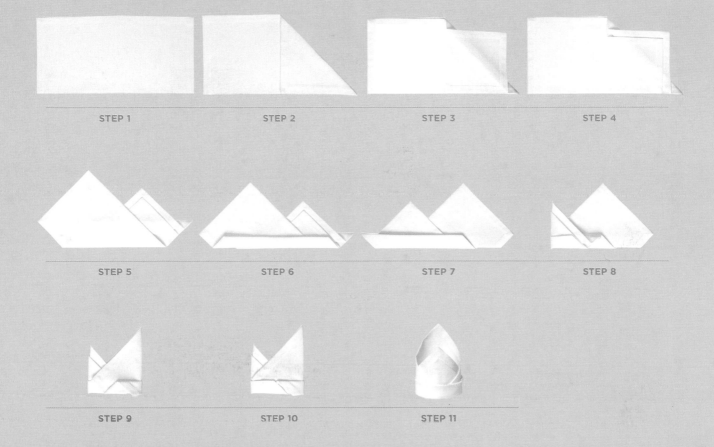

STEP 1    STEP 2    STEP 3    STEP 4

STEP 5    STEP 6    STEP 7    STEP 8

STEP 9    STEP 10    STEP 11

**4.** Repeat the step with the bottom layer, leaving about 1 inch of space between them so that the top layer does not completely cover the bottom layer.

**5.** Fold the lower left corner up until it is about 1 inch higher than the point on the right. Rotate the napkin to the left. The napkin should be straight along the bottom and at the top; it will resemble two "mountain peaks," the taller one on the left.

**6.** Fold the bottom edge up, creating a 2-inch band along the bottom. Press.

**7.** Flip the entire napkin over, with the longest edge of the napkin still at the bottom and the smaller of the two "mountain peaks" on the left.

**8.** Vertically fold the left side of the napkin to the right so that the left "mountain" is folded in half.

**9.** Repeat in reverse on the right, vertically folding the larger "mountain" in half on top of the left fold.

**10.** Tuck the base of the upper layer into the folds of the band of the lower layer.

**11.** Stand the napkin upright after opening the band to create a circle resembling the base of a crown.

# Head of the Class

**THE GRADUATION FOLD**

Most napkin folds can be made to fit a number of occasions. Change the fabric, print, or setting, and *voilà!* the fold fits. But the Graduation Fold should be reserved for one event and one event only—the day that celebrates years of a job well done. Still, a change of tassel color or color of fabric can give the fold plenty of dignified variety. A soft white or ivory napkin looks sharp and offers a touch of class (pun intended). On the other hand, selecting a vivid print or plaid brings a festive aura. After an afternoon of pomp and circumstance, a lively bit of mirth can be fitting and welcome.

**POMP AND CIRCUMSTANCE:** While the napkin doesn't require a tassel, or even a button, these touches give the Graduation Fold napkin a distinctive charm. A short, flowing ribbon can also be used. The starkness of this black-and-white setting, featuring a bright white napkin, button, and tassel atop a dark charger, conveys a sense of dignity appropriate to the celebration of a milestone achievement.

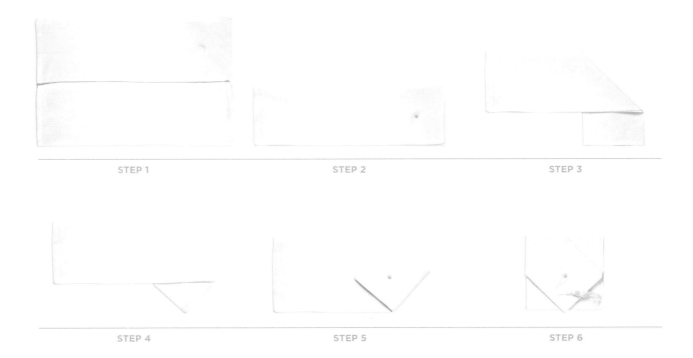

STEP 1                    STEP 2                    STEP 3

STEP 4                    STEP 5                    STEP 6

**ADDITIONAL MATERIALS NEEDED:**
tassels, small knotted or ball-shape buttons, thread to match, sewing needle

**NOTE:** Sew a button onto the napkin (we've used a small, knotted button shaped like a ball). To position the button, completely fold one test napkin and mark the center of the "mortarboard" with an erasable fabric pencil or pin. Open the napkin and mark that same spot on all the napkins. Sew one button on that mark on each napkin.

**1.** Begin with the napkin fully open, laid out as a square, button side down, with the button positioned on the underside of the upper right corner. Visually divide the napkin into thirds and fold the bottom third of the napkin horizontally up onto the middle third.

**2.** Horizontally fold the upper third of the napkin down to make a wide rectangle. You will now see the button on the right. Press.

**3.** With a thumb holding the napkin at the center top edge, fold the right half of the napkin under itself and pull down so that it extends about 3 inches below the bottom of the rectangle. Press.

**4.** On the 3-inch flap that extends below the rectangle, fold both corners up to meet in the middle and along the bottom of the rectangle. Press.

## GO GET 'EM, TIGER!

Mortarboards worn by today's graduates evolved over the centuries from square, cloth-covered hats worn by educators in medieval times. More recently, each field of academia has become associated with a specific color tassel. To give the Graduation Fold an extra touch of personality, color coordinate the tassel to match the graduate's major field of study.

Agriculture = Maize

Architecture = Violet

Arts/Letters/Humanities = White

Consumer science = Maroon

Doctorate degrees = Gold

Economics = Copper

Education = Light blue

Engineering = Orange

Journalism = Crimson

Law = Purple

Medicine = Green

Music = Pink

Nursing = Apricot

Philosophy = Dark blue

Physical education = Sage green

Public health = Salmon

Science = Golden yellow

Theology = Scarlet

**5.** Holding the newly folded two corners in place, turn that part of the napkin up so that the far-right corner meets the top corner of the 45-degree angle. This forms a diamond shape with a button in the center on the right side of the rectangle. Press.

**6.** Making sure to keep the mortarboard in place with your right hand, carefully lift it, and with your left hand, fold the left side of the rectangle completely under the mortarboard so that it creates a square behind the diamond. Press. Attach the tassel to the button.

# A Breeze

## THE KITE FOLD

For a flight of fancy, few folds fit the bill better than a sprightly kite festooned with a sassy tail. Bright bold stripes or prints help to set the design aloft. The kite is a natural for children's parties and also works for spring-theme gatherings or picnic-style luncheons—anywhere the attitude is fun and light. And that includes baby showers. In some Far Eastern cultures, tradition holds that after a baby is born, kites are flown and let go as a way to shoo bad spirits up, up, and away.

**AN AIR OF AMUSEMENT:** The stripes on the napkin gleefully run in opposite directions, with the napkin's folded side kept face up to make the most of the dazzling mix of colors. A matching yellow ribbon creates the tail, adorned with tiny ribbon bows of a contrasting color attached with a glue gun. Stitched to the kite's lower corner, the ribbon dangles with disarming insouciance.

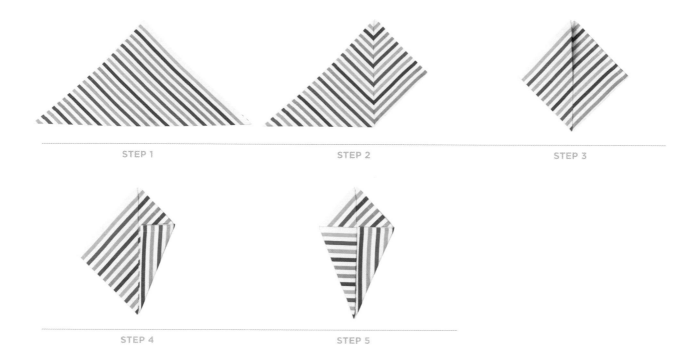

STEP 1

STEP 2

STEP 3

STEP 4

STEP 5

**ADDITIONAL MATERIALS NEEDED:**
skinny ribbon or stiff paper for
bows, thin ribbon or yarn for the
tail, hot glue gun, sewing needle,
thread to match tail, scissors

**1.** Begin with the napkin fully open, laid out as a diamond, then fold it
in half to make a triangle with the folded edge at the bottom. Press.

**2.** Hold one finger at the exact center of the bottom fold and, with
the other hand, move the right corner to meet the tip of the
triangle.

**3.** Repeat with the left corner, creating a diamond shape with a pair of
folds forming a line down the middle. Press.

**4.** Hold the bottom corner down with one finger and, with the other
hand, bring the right corner to the middle folds of the diamond.

**5.** Repeat with the left corner, creating a kite shape. Press. To complete
the kite, read on.

*To make the kite's tail:* Cut a strand of thin ribbon or yarn about 3 feet long.

*To make the bows:* Cut several 1-inch strips from skinny ribbon or stiff paper. To make sure the bows are evenly shaped, fold ribbon or paper in half, cut the strips, and then open them.

With a glue gun, attach the bows along the tail, about 2 inches apart. Attach one end of the tail to the lower corner of the kite with 2 or 3 simple stitches, being careful to maintain the shape of the kite.

Place the napkin in the center of the place setting, either letting the tail drape over the table's edge or letting it curve playfully, as though someone has let go of the string and the kite is making its escape.

**KITE DAY:** By choosing a clever napkin fold, a theme is set for the entire table and even the event itself—anyone for a little game of pin the tail on the kite? The kite tails are draped over the edge of each plate and then the table itself. Smaller paper kites, each with its own tail, are place cards rising out from among the blades of a low wheatgrass centerpiece dotted with black-eyed Susans (the grass is bordered by bright yellow ribbon pinned around the edge to hide the soil). Multicolored tumblers add to the aura of spring.

# Flashbulb

## THE TULIP FOLD

Whether spring has arrived or is just a state of mind, tulips epitomize the season. But that doesn't mean the all-season Tulip Fold has to be saved for an April event. It works wonders in the middle of winter to help you forget about the cold and nicely rounds out summer tables, whether dining alfresco, indoors at a wedding shower luncheon, or at any lighthearted get-together. Winter, spring, summer, fall, a table full of linen flowers will brighten the day, especially if detailed with leafy stems that can also serve as cheery place cards. Choose napkins in solid bold colors—chartreuse, violet, orange—to give the fold an extra-rich touch of whimsy.

**TULIPOMANIA:** Flowered dinnerware and tablecloths match the ebullience of the Tulip Fold. When adding a fabric stem to the fold, tuck the upper part into the blossom and let the leaves drape across the plate or place setting.

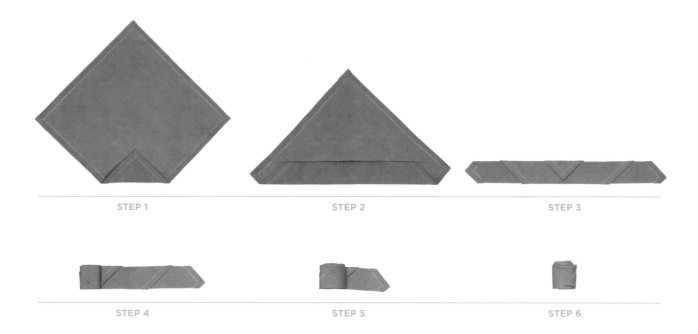

STEP 1    STEP 2    STEP 3

STEP 4    STEP 5    STEP 6

**ADDITIONAL MATERIALS NEEDED:**
green fabric, yellow embroidery
floss, embroidery needle, paper
for pattern, scissors, pencil

**1.** Begin with the napkin fully open, laid out as a diamond, then fold
the lower point up and crease along the bottom edge.

**2.** Fold the folded edge up 3 inches and crease along the bottom.

**3.** Continue folding up the folded edge in 3-inch increments so that
you end up with a band about 3 inches wide, with the final napkin
point on top. Press.

**4.** Beginning at one end, roll the band and create a hole in the middle
about the size of a roll of quarters (about 1 inch in diameter). The
roll should be compact but not too tight.

**5.** Roll until there are 3 or 4 inches of the band left unrolled.

**6.** Tuck the unrolled end into an open edge on the outside of the
band. Take time with this, as the tucked part, representing "petals,"
will show.

From the top of the roll, working one layer at a time, gently pull up
the inner two layers of the band so that about ½ inch of each layer
is visible.

**STEMWARE:** The tulip's easily crafted stem, which is stitched together using a hand-drawn template, also serves as a place card. Here, bright green fabric is contrasted with yellow topstitching that edges the leaves and stem, and spells out each guest's name. Another option is to simply cut the stem and leaves from green construction paper and use a marker for the names—it's easy and looks just as sweet.

**BLOOM IN LOVE:** Three examples of the Tulip Fold, sans stems, clearly illustrate the derivation of the word *tulip,* from the Turkish word for "turban." Though white is always appropriate, bright colors play up the fold's floral pizzazz.

# Hop to It

## THE BUNNY FOLD

After an afternoon of egg coloring, egg rolling, and egg hunting, the Easter parade eventually marches to the dining room in search of sustenance. And when it gets there, why not greet it with a happy-faced Bunny Fold napkin sporting jelly bean eyes and licorice whiskers? The fold is a charming complement to an Easter-theme luncheon and much less ironic than serving, say, *pâté de lapin*. The fold is ultra simple, so it's no problem even if you need to make it by the dozen (you know how easily bunnies multiply).

**A GOOD EGG:** With decorated eggs in egg cups serving as place cards, an Easter table is a colorful field of dots and dashes starring the Bunny Fold. Jelly bean eyes and nose, and licorice whiskers and mouth, make for one cute bunny. The shape of the napkin is so obviously "rabbity" that it doesn't need the extra touches, though no one would blame you if you gave one of the ears a casual flop.

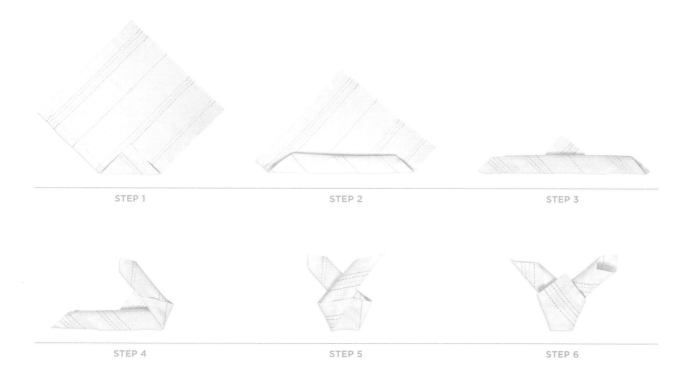

STEP 1           STEP 2           STEP 3

STEP 4           STEP 5           STEP 6

**ADDITIONAL MATERIALS NEEDED (OPTIONAL):** jelly beans, licorice strings, and any other fun candies

1. Begin with the napkin fully open, laid out as a diamond, then fold up the lower point 3 or 4 inches and crease the fold with your fingers along the bottom. The thinner the band, the longer the bunny's "ears."

2. Fold the folded edge up 3 or 4 inches and crease the fold with your fingers along the bottom.

3. Continue folding up the folded edge, stopping 3 or 4 inches from the top. Press.

4. Fold the right side of the napkin band up along the right edge of the triangle so that it overlaps the bottom layer by about 4 inches.

5. Repeat with the left side of the band, pointing it toward 2 o'clock (if you visualize a clock face). Press.

6. Flip the napkin over. *There's your bunny.*

## SETTING THE HALLOWEEN TABLE

When preparing the table for a Halloween celebration, you want to focus more on treats than tricks. The last thing guests want to see are gruesome decorations of blood and gore or centerpieces festooned with Jason's hockey mask staring back at them. (Still, we can't have anything but fond memories of the Halloween party given a few years back when the host jokingly put one apple at each place setting, complete with a protruding razor blade. Bless him.) Set the mood with delightful reminders of the fun side of the season.

- Place a single, large jack-o'-lantern in the middle of the table on a plush nest of tumbles of minipumpkins interwoven with bittersweet vines and autumn leaves. Intersperse with votives for additional sparkle.

- Instead of a jack-o'-lantern face, carve fanciful designs all around a single large pumpkin, using a melon baller, apple corer, knife, or other implements. Try a stunning abstract pattern, such as baroque scrolls, odd geometric designs, or simple polka dots. No need even to carve all the way through the pumpkin skin, as simply scooping out varying layers will create the look of orange-frosted glass.

- On an inexpensive orange tablecloth (or a large piece of orange fabric), center a large spiderweb drawn with a black marker. A sophisticated alternative would be to use fine black silk thread to create the web on orange taffeta, another example of how elegance can obliterate kitsch.

- Serve cider, pumpkin bread or pie, candied apples, or other fall holiday foods. Consider a first course of pumpkin soup served in small carved-out pumpkins instead of bowls.

- After the meal—séance optional.

# A Friendly Ghost

## THE GHOST FOLD

Halloween doesn't have to be spooky; it can also be a hoot. Not that there's anything wrong with scary music, grim settings, and characters that make your skin crawl—goodness knows we've seen *Phantom of the Opera* more times than we can count. For Halloween feasts, though, it's nice to accentuate the fun. That's where the Ghost Fold comes in, a bubbly apparition looking for just the right place setting to haunt. While it is definitely appropriate for the younger set, don't forget that adults, too, love the iconography of holidays. Using a fine, white gossamer linen or organdy napkin removes the kitsch factor of the fold and helps create the ghostly illusion. Hand-embroidered eyes and a necklace of satin ribbon elevate the ghost to a chic wink to the season.

STEP 1                 STEP 2                 STEP 3

**1.** Drape the napkin over the balloon (see Note). Gather the napkin around the balloon, being sure the eyes are properly positioned. Wrap a matching piece of narrow ribbon around the base of the balloon and loosely tie a bow. Do not tie the bow too tightly because you will later need to pull out the deflated balloon through the opening. Besides, giving it a wider "neck" will make it look more like a ghost.

**2.** With a needle, carefully pop the balloon, delicately handling the napkin so that the napkin-shape "head" of the ghost remains intact. Carefully slip the deflated balloon out through the neck opening.

**3.** Prop the ghost on a wineglass or champagne flute so that it "floats" over the place setting.

**ADDITIONAL MATERIALS NEEDED:** black embroidery thread, balloons (any color), narrow white ribbon

**NOTE:** Before you start, stitch a small pair of eyes near the center of your napkin. The eyes can simply be two dots, or if you want to do something more intricate, you can sew in lashes and pupils. Inflate a balloon to a diameter of about 4 inches and tie it closed. Holding the balloon by the tied end, place the balloon (the head) behind the napkin so the eyes are centered on the front.

# Special Delivery

## THE ENVELOPE FOLD

In these days of three-way paging and instant messaging, an elegant envelope recalls a gentler time when a proper invitation arrived only by mail. Many thoughtful touches of the past too often get lost in our fast-track lives, but you can still send a message of kind regards that's sincerely yours, even if you don't have time to handwrite every invitation. The Envelope Fold is simple and quick, a small effort that clearly delivers. Want to take the design a step further? An embroidered flap helps seal the deal. For extra fun, consider placing a little note in each guest's napkin—perhaps a note that offers a bit of interesting information about the diner sitting across the table, something to serve as an icebreaker.

**THE ENVELOPE, PLEASE:** The meal begins on a sweet note with the envelope's flap cheerily announcing "Bon Appétit!" in embroidered letters. Wooden letters, available at hobby shops, playfully edge the dinner plate and act as place card holders. The letters, along with a tablecloth emblazoned with celebratory words, round out a theme of warm greetings. Inside the napkins we've placed a brief handwritten note personalized for each guest. Expect a stamp of approval.

**NOTE:** As photographed here and on page 99, the napkin was embroidered before being folded.

1. Begin with the napkin fully open, laid out as a square, then vertically fold the right edge in to the center line. Press.

2. Repeat the fold from the left edge.

3. Fold the bottom edge up to the center line of the rectangle.

4. Repeat with the upper half so that what were the top and bottom edges now meet in the middle. Press.

5. Fold the upper two corners inward until they meet in the middle at the crease line, which will make a point at the top. This is the envelope's flap. Press.

6. Fold the flap down onto the napkin. Press. *First class.*

# Party Like It's 1999
## THE WHITE HOUSE FOLD, 1999

From the Kennedy era through the presidency of George H. W. Bush, the cuisine of the White House was predominantly French. Even when Gerald Ford insisted on serving wines from his home state of Michigan (a choice not well received in some circles), the kitchen remained French. That all changed when Bill and Hillary Clinton moved into the executive mansion and switched the emphasis to regional American fare. When hosting state dinners for the King of Morocco or the presidents of the Philippines, the Republic of South Africa, or Argentina—all official guests of the Clintons in 1999—there was an equally dignified menu that still had plenty of exuberance. It was a statement furthered by their choice of napkin fold, which was used throughout the year. Here's my interpretation.

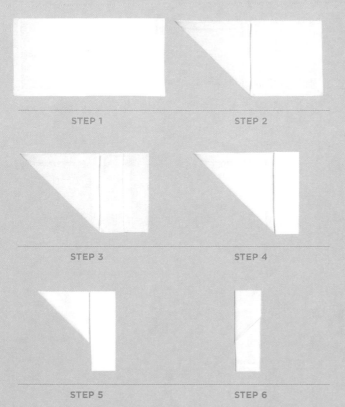

STEP 1

STEP 2

STEP 3

STEP 4

STEP 5

STEP 6

1. Begin with the napkin fully open, laid out as a square, then fold it in half horizontally, so that the fold is at the top. Press.

2. Fold the lower left corner up until it meets the top folded edge in the middle of the napkin so that you have a triangular fold on the left and a square on the right. Press.

3. Fold the right edge of the square portion of the napkin to the center line of the square.

4. Again, fold the right edge one third to the left to meet the edge of the triangle.

5. Vertically fold the panel to the left on top of the triangle.

6. Fold the remaining part of the triangle to the right, wrapping the loose point around the back of the panel. Press.

# Napkin$^2$

## THE ELEGANT SQUARE FOLD

Sometimes something is so square, it's hip. The Elegant Square is a case in point: Its pure minimalism is blatantly abstract yet arrestingly obvious, an ultimate understatement of mathematical beauty. The formula works well in the confined space of a place setting, perhaps at a table complemented by an uncomplicated clutch of calla lilies in a clear glass vase. Someone please let Calvin Klein know his invitation is in the mail.

**IT'S HIP TO BE SQUARE:** The Elegant Square is so deceivingly simple that one might be forgiven for not even noticing that it's a fold at all. The simplicity requires that each step of the fold be followed meticulously. Here, precisely centered on a square plate, the exactingly folded napkin coolly reiterates the geometry of the tablecloth's hemstitched grid.

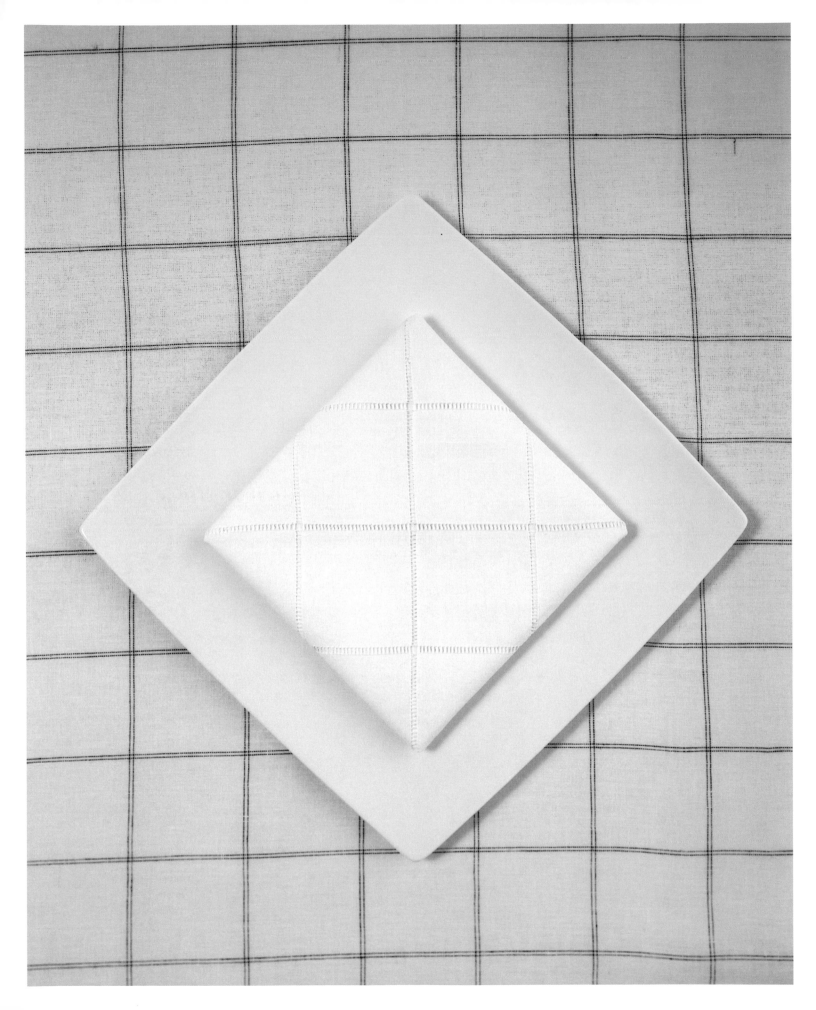

**BETWEEN THE LINES:** The strict form of the Elegant Square can be deceptive. Released from its archly formal fold, the napkin is revealed as inviting, soft, and delicate.

**1.** With the napkin fully open, laid out as a square, bring the bottom of the napkin up and the top down to meet in a horizontal line in the middle. Press.

**2.** Fold the left edge to the center line of the rectangle. Press.

**3.** Repeat the fold on the right so that both edges meet in the middle. Press.

**4.** Fold both top corners down to meet at the center line. Press.

**5.** Fold both bottom corners up to meet at the center line. Press.

**6.** Carefully hold the middle of the napkin and flip the napkin over. *Squaresville.*

# Serviette de La Vallée
## THE RESTAURANT MICHEL BRAS FOLD

After the late-spring snows have melted in the tiny town of Laguiole in the Aubrac region of southwest France, a legendary restaurant opens its doors for the season. For those who've had the foresight to make a reservation two months beforehand, a stop at Restaurant Michel Bras will not go unrewarded. With signature dishes such as lobster with leeks and desserts that include hot biscuits filled with gooey bittersweet chocolate, the restaurant—open only from April to October—has been acclaimed as one of the world's finest. Using local herbs, meats, and vegetables, owner and chef Michel Bras has created an impossibly popular culinary destination far from the beaten path. Among the napkin folds he uses is this slim diamond shape.

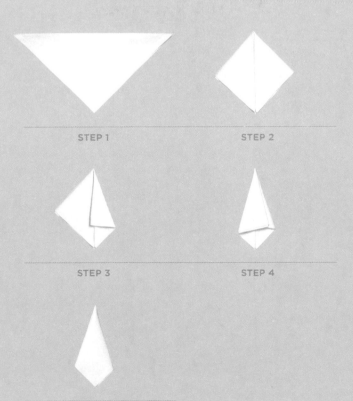

STEP 1

STEP 2

STEP 3

STEP 4

STEP 5

**OPTIONAL MATERIALS:** small stainless-steel rings

1. Begin with the napkin fully open, laid out as a diamond, then fold the top point down to meet the bottom point, creating a triangle with the folded edge at the top.

2. Fold the right and left corners of the triangle down to the bottom point, creating a diamond shape with a vertical slit down the middle. Press.

3. Holding down the top point with one hand, with the other hand, fold the right corner across the vertical slit so that the point lies about 1 inch to the left of the slit.

4. Repeat step 3, folding the left corner on top of the right-side fold so that the point lies about 1 inch to the right side of the slit. Press.

5. Turn the napkin over. (Optional: To do as the restaurant does, slip a small stainless-steel ring over the top point and slide it down about 3 inches from the point.)

# The Sophisticates

## THE TAPER FOLD

Pretty is as pretty does. A table of fine china, sterling silver flatware, leaded crystal, and a luxuriant centerpiece requires an appropriately refined napkin that will not draw attention away from the place setting. The chic, clean lines of the Taper Fold hit just that right note. Think of it as a night on the town when you're dressed to the nines and you're trying to decide on accessories. Your choice needs to be appropriate to the event, avoiding anything ostentatious or loud that might outshine the overall look. It's also a shape that beautifully displays a napkin's fine embroidery or monogram.

**THAT'S AN UNDERSTATEMENT:** A sumptuous table underscores, but is in no way overwhelmed by, the Taper Fold's streamlined silhouette. The shape's simplicity ensures that nothing distracts from the star power of the centerpiece, while still providing a suitable platform for a napkin that possesses outstanding embroidery, lace, or a monogram. The setting's hushed formality is further assured by sitting place cards—with names written in hand-penned cursive—squarely atop the napkin.

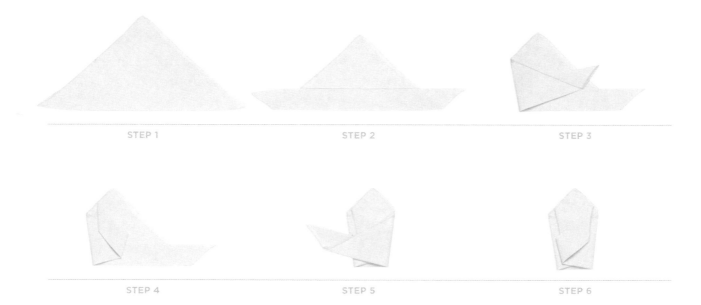

STEP 1    STEP 2    STEP 3

STEP 4    STEP 5    STEP 6

STEP 7

1. Begin with the napkin fully open, laid out in a diamond, then fold it in half into a triangle with the fold at the bottom.

2. Fold the bottom edge up 3 inches to create a wide band at the triangle's base. Press.

3. Grasp the lower left corner of the napkin and fold it over to the right side so that the bottom edge of the left side of the band meets the top edge of the right side of the band. Imagine the face of a clock, with noon at the top. After folding, the lower left corner points to 2 o'clock, while the right side of the band points to 3 o'clock. The left point extends outside the edge of the triangle.

4. Fold the band pointing to 2 o'clock over onto itself so that it points to 11 o'clock and the tip does not extend beyond the napkin's edge. Press.

5. Grasp the right side of the band pointing to 3 o'clock and fold it across the napkin so that it points to 10 o'clock.

6. Fold the band pointing to 10 o'clock over onto itself so that the tip does not extend beyond the napkin's edge. Press.

7. Carefully turn over the napkin and place it with the point toward your guest.

# Well Done and Rare
## THE DELMONICO'S FOLD

Delmonico's, the venerated New York restaurant located a stone's throw from Wall Street, was likely the nation's first true restaurant and certainly the undisputed home of truly fine dining. When it opened in the early 1800s, America was still a nascent democracy where the closest thing to a real restaurant was a tavern or roadhouse. That all changed with the opening of Delmonico's Restaurant & Steak House. Amazingly, the menu ran more than 100 pages in length and featured nearly 400 dishes, the cellar held 16,000 bottles of wine, and the pillars at the entrance had been unearthed and transported from Pompeii. Among its famous diners of the era were Ulysses Grant and Charles Dickens. Almost 200 years later, the restaurant is still a stunning dining experience, with tables that feature an ultra-simple, fastidiously folded square napkin.

STEP 1    STEP 2    STEP 3    STEP 4

**1.** Begin with the napkin fully open, laid out as a square, then fold it in half horizontally, so that the folded edge is at the top. Press.

**2.** Vertically fold the left edge to the center of the napkin.

**3.** Vertically fold the right edge to the center so that the two edges meet in the middle. Press.

**4.** Flip the napkin over, keeping the folded edge on top. *Found at the best tables!*

# Inside Job

## THE POCKET FOLD

A nosegay tucked into a Pocket Fold napkin is a thoughtful offering and a fetching touch. Throughout the evening, you'll spy guests raising the bouquet to their noses, and at evening's end, they'll have a charming souvenir to take home. Vary the contents of the bouquet with anything from flowers to feathers, foliage to herbs, or a combination. Or the pocket could hold something entirely different—a candy cane at the holidays, a small remembrance, the menu, a personal note, a photograph, or something as simple as silverware.

**A POCKET FULL OF POSIES:** The Pocket Fold translates well for formal as well as casual affairs and can be fine-tuned with various floral selections and arrangements. A fanciful cluster of summer's bounty colorfully fills the napkin and crowns the place setting with a flourish.

STEP 1

STEP 2

STEP 3

STEP 4

STEP 5

**ADDITIONAL MATERIALS NEEDED:** fresh flowers, ribbon to match napkin, scissors

**NOTE:** Prepare bouquets in advance by gathering together a small collection of flowers (or other items suitable for the bouquet) and tying them together with a matching ribbon. Keep them in water until just before dinner is served. When you are ready to use them, pat them dry and slip them into the napkins.

**1.** Begin with the napkin fully open, laid out as a square, then fold it horizontally so that the top edge meets the center of the napkin. Press.

**2.** Fold the bottom edge under so that it meets the center line on the underside of the napkin.

**3.** Fold the right edge of the napkin vertically to meet the center of the napkin.

**4.** Repeat with the left side so that the two outer edges meet in the center. Press.

**5.** Vertically fold the napkin in half. Press.

# California Dreamy
## THE FRENCH LAUNDRY FOLD

Somewhere between Napa and Nirvana stands The French Laundry, a culinary outpost that many consider the finest restaurant in America (*Restaurant Magazine* selected it as the best restaurant *in the world* in 2004). Located deep in northern California's wine country within a rustic century-old former steam laundry, The French Laundry serves contemporary American fare with French influences, though some call it nothing less than sheer heaven. With creations as intricate as poached moulard duck foie gras au torchon, chef Thomas Keller has established a restaurant almost without peer. The restaurant's signature—a clothespin that pinches the table's crisply layered napkin—was my inspiration.

STEP 1

STEP 2

STEP 3

STEP 4

**ADDITIONAL MATERIALS NEEDED:** clothespins

1. Begin with the napkin fully open, laid out as a diamond, then fold the top point down to create a triangle with the folded edge at the top.

2. Fold the triangle in half vertically by bringing the left corner to the right corner. Press.

3. Imagine a clock, with the napkin's right corner pointing to 3 and the bottom corner to 6. With one hand holding the upper left corner in place, grasp only the top layers of the right corner and fold them down so that the corner points to 5 o'clock.

4. Now grasp the remaining upper right corner and fold it down so that the corner points to about 4 o'clock. The three points of the corners should be equidistant from one another. Press.

5. To complete the French Laundry look, at the top, use a clothespin to clasp the two bottom layers, hiding it under the fold of the top layer.

# Western Brand

### THE COWBOY FOLD

When the chuck wagon rustles up a heap of vittles, the Cowboy Fold sets a mood even the most ornery ranch hand can appreciate. Though strictly for affairs that are at home on the range, it's a fold impressive enough for city slickers, too, perhaps evoking memories of a week at a dude ranch. Beyond the fold itself, the kerchief slide—the band that will corral the two ends of the fold together—can also serve as a decorative element. The Cowboy Fold is ideal for Western-theme parties, of course, but the item you select to hold the fold together can make it a good match for other events as well.

Store-bought napkin rings work fine as kerchief slides for the Cowboy Fold, but also try other ideas that might serve double duty as party favors.

- Pacifier—think baby shower
- Jewelry—anything from costume jewelry rings with oversize baubles (engagement party?) to a fine double-layer bracelet
- Pine or cedar twigs woven into a circle—nice for winter
- Hardware—oversize nuts (as in nuts and bolts), washers, or a short length of coil lend a masculine theme
- Dry pasta—a tube of manicotti or cannelloni adds a rustic Tuscan touch

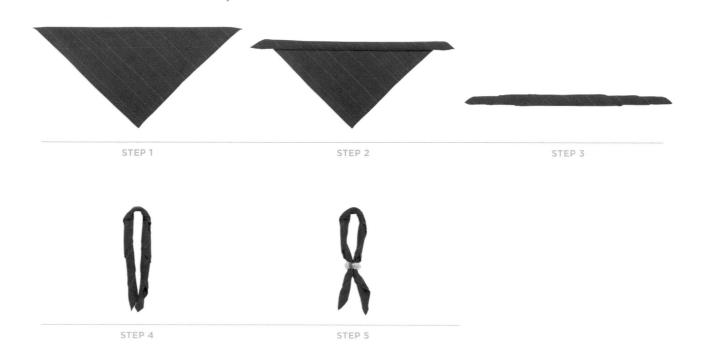

STEP 1         STEP 2         STEP 3

STEP 4         STEP 5

**1.** Begin with the napkin fully open, laid out as a diamond, then fold the top point down to meet the bottom point, creating a triangle with the folded edge at the top. Press.

**2.** Working from the top folded edge to the bottom point, make a 1-inch-wide roll.

**3.** Continue rolling downward until the entire napkin is rolled.

**4.** Bend the roll in half.

**5.** Hold the two ends of the roll together, creating a loop, at the same time that you spread open the top of the loop. Using a kerchief slide that easily, though not loosely, fits around both ends, slide it about halfway up the roll. Spread the two ends apart to convey the impression of a kerchief.

**ADDITIONAL MATERIALS NEEDED:**
kerchief slides or napkin rings

# Roll Play

## THE NAPKIN ROLLS

Not on a roll, in a roll. When you are serving buffet style, each guest must carry his or her utensils, napkins, and plate(s) of food (and occasionally a beverage as well). Securing the flatware inside a Napkin Roll helps with the balancing act as guests make their way through the buffet line. The rolls themselves are secured by napkin "rings" made from materials that are as varied as your choice of appetizers and entrées. For example, starched white linen napkins held in place with matching white linen bands lend an air of elegance to a formal setting, whereas a bold floral pattern enlivens a garden party. Accessorize with any number of doodads—buttons, pins, clips, buckles, snaps, anything really—to make the setting unique.

**BUCKLED DOWN:** A buffet gets the plush treatment with silverware wrapped within tight Napkin Rolls belted in brown-stitched bands looped through dark wood buckles.

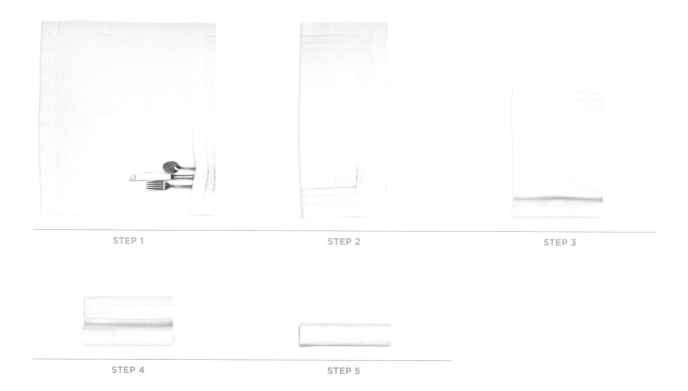

STEP 1    STEP 2    STEP 3

STEP 4    STEP 5

**ADDITIONAL MATERIALS NEEDED:**
napkin rings or ribbons, buckles, buttons and matching thread, sewing needle

**1.** Begin with the napkin fully open, laid out as a square, then vertically fold the right side in about 3 inches. Press. Tuck flatware inside the folded edge.

**2.** Vertically fold the left side of the napkin so that it meets the edge of the right side and completely covers the flatware.

**3.** Carefully flip over the napkin. Beginning at the bottom of the napkin, tightly roll the napkin toward the top, enclosing the flatware in the roll. Leave about 4 inches of the napkin unrolled.

**4.** Fold the top edge down about 2 inches.

**5.** Complete the roll.

Craft a napkin "ring" (see page 119) that will fit snuggly around the napkin roll and slip the ring over the napkin. *Ring and roll.*

## WHAT WILL YOU USE TO BAND YOUR NAPKIN ROLL?

The choices are limited only by your imagination. Look for unusual fabrics and consider offbeat sources to create a look that's yours alone.

- Did you happen to save a leftover piece of the wallpaper that covers your dining room walls? Trim it into 2-inch-wide bands to loop around your napkins (and see if any guests notice).

- Inscribe lengths of parchment with a special note ("Love is the food of life."—Shakespeare) written in fancy script.

- For a stylish touch, stitch a tassel to a fabric ring or tuck a small rosebud inside the band.

- Nautical theme? Try doughnut-shape plastic foam rings, available at craft stores, decorated as life preservers (SS *Mess Hall*?).

- Bikers on the guest list might enjoy napkins cuffed in leather and secured with grommets. Oh, who are we kidding? Everyone will enjoy that.

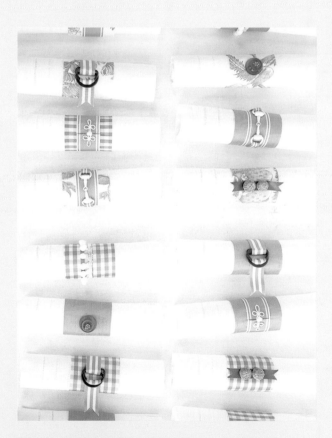

**ROLL CALL:** Rows of Napkin Rolls show variations on a springtime theme of green. Fabric and ribbon "rings" hold rolled napkins in place, while a wide array of buckles, belts, buttons, bows, and other elements gives each roll its own statement, varying from casual to highbrow.

**TRUSS ME:** With the help of a small plastic buckle, a playfully striped ribbon is lassoed to duty as a napkin belt.

# Pleated Elegance

## THE TRI-FOLD

A well-folded napkin can make any occasion special, but what if the occasion is already special? We're talking about a visiting head of state or, perhaps, the world's most finicky in-laws. The simple repetition of three evenly placed folds, crisply defined with the touch of a steam iron, is the ultimate in quiet chic, whether it's a sit-down dinner for one hundred following a formal evening wedding or a regal gathering of the couple's closest friends. It's also a great opportunity to highlight a particularly recherché pattern or design, such as heirloom lace, dainty embroidery, or hand-stitched monograms.

**THE LAYERED LOOK:** The three evenly spaced folds of the Tri-Fold set a tone that's repeated in each fine detail of this luxurious table. Fine china, leaded crystal, and a sumptuous rose centerpiece comfortably share space in a place setting that is just this side of divine. The folds are elemental beauty personified—ideal for featuring delicate handiwork, but they can also be used to unobtrusively hold a place card, personal note, or perhaps a charming antique postcard commemorating the event.

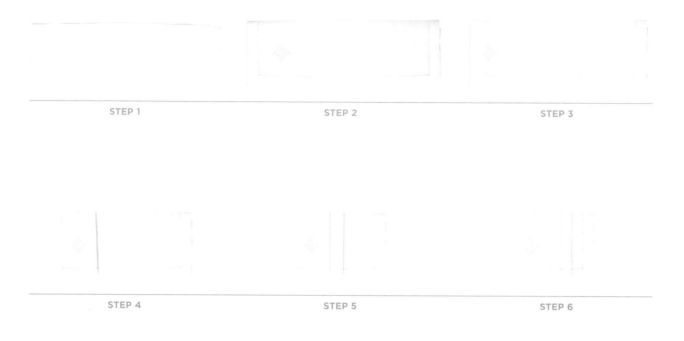

STEP 1        STEP 2        STEP 3

STEP 4        STEP 5        STEP 6

STEP 7

1. Begin with the napkin fully open, laid out as a square, then fold the bottom edge up equal to one third of the total height of the napkin. Press.

2. Fold the top edge down on top of the already-folded third so that the top layer covers the bottom layers and the edges meet.

3. Fold the left edge back and under approximately 2 inches.

4. Lift the left side and fold it onto itself approximately 3 inches to create the first pleat. (You may find it easier to turn the napkin vertically while making the pleats.)

5. Carefully lift the first pleat and the area of the napkin just below it and create a second pleat by making another vertical fold about 1 inch to the right of the first, again, pleating it in to itself.

6. Repeat the process until you have three equally spaced pleats. Press.

7. Tuck the remaining part of the napkin under itself to create a fourth and final pleat the same width as the others. Press. *Mission com-pleat.*

# "A Wisp of Glory Called Camelot"
## THE KENNEDY WHITE HOUSE FOLD

The thousand days of the John F. Kennedy presidency were a whirlwind of history and controversy, and they introduced the White House to a new era of American style and grace. Much of the Kennedy mystique was created by the president's wife, a woman who even made wearing faux pearls a fashion statement. Jacqueline Kennedy's assured presence, beguiling beauty, and regal bearing put schoolchildren at ease and charmed world leaders. French President Charles de Gaulle may have dared to question her husband, but when it came to Jackie, he was just another docile pup. Only thirty-one years of age when she became First Lady (a term she disliked), Jackie's elegance and breeding became the modern standard of good taste. The thin, spare lines of the Kennedy White House Fold epitomize that unaffected elegance. Following is my adaptation of this fold.

| STEP 1 | STEP 2 | STEP 3 | STEP 4 |

**1.** Begin with the napkin fully open, laid out as a square, then fold it in half horizontally so that the fold is at the top.

**2.** Fold the napkin in half vertically so that the left side is on top, creating a square. Press.

**3.** Fold the right side to the left one third of the total width of the napkin.

**4.** Fold the left third to the right so that the left edge lies on top of the right folded edge. Press. *Slender and refined.*

# Wrap Party

### THE COZY FOLD

When the menu is just beverages, the Cozy Fold keeps things uncomplicated by wrapping the napkin directly around the libation. Like water pipes and people, the Cozy Fold runs hot and cold. Wrap it around the world's coldest beverage and it stops that feeling of frostbite at the same time that it insulates an icy, tall drink of water (ahem, yes, er . . . *water!*). Conversely, when a friendly bout of sudden-death ice hockey breaks out on the backyard pond, cuddle it around a mug of hot cider or cocoa and beverages stay warm. And as a consolation to the loser: free refills!

**BUNDLE OF JOY:** A cup of hot cocoa topped with a tasty dollop of whipped cream is nestled within a trusty Cozy Fold. Besides keeping the cocoa warm, it will catch little slips of the sip and, after the mittens come off, protect delicate fingertips from the heat.

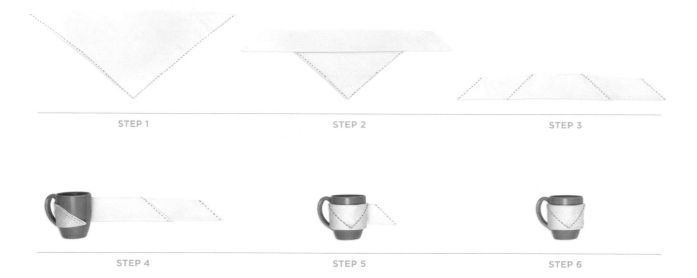

STEP 1     STEP 2     STEP 3

STEP 4     STEP 5     STEP 6

**NOTE:** Think small. This fold works only with lunch-size napkins (16 inches by 16 inches).

**1.** Begin with the napkin fully open, laid out as a diamond, then fold it in half to form a triangle with the fold at the top. Press.

**2.** Fold the folded edge down to the middle of the triangle.

**3.** Fold the bottom point of the triangle up and tuck it under the band.

**4.** Place the napkin on a mug and thread the left end of the band through the mug handle as though you were putting a belt through a loop.

**5.** Continue to wrap the napkin around the mug until only a 3- to 4-inch tail remains.

**6.** Tuck the tail into the layer closest to it to create a totally smooth fold. *Piping hot!*

## GETTING COZY IN THE LONE STAR STATE

The summer side of the Cozy Fold can be found in the heart of Texas, where keeping a cold beverage protected from the stifling heat is a top priority. In some parts of the state, ordering a bottle of beer produces a tall cold one by a barkeep who carefully wraps a paper napkin around each bottle, producing some of the finest folds this side of . . . well, Texas. Each bar has its own style of paper napkin cozy— folded once, wrapped, and then tucked under; wrapped and then folded over; wrapped around the neck like a kerchief and looped once—and each style has its own rate of success at staying put. The paper napkins don't really do that much to keep the beer cold, but like the state itself, they're just so darn friendly. Adding to the lore are the amusing names given to these meticulous sinecures, including "handkerchiefs," "diapers," "Huggies," and "bibs."

**NIGHT OF CUPS:** Cozy Folds keep a tray of marshmallow-topped hot chocolate feeling snuggly. The napkins are useful in keeping the cups warm and fingers protected, and they also are an attractive decoration.

# Made in Japan

## THE SUSHI FOLD

The cool stylings of the Far East take shape in a compact, rolled napkin that's minimal in design yet tastefully bold in presentation. Like the surprisingly rich flavor of a chilled wedge of yellowtail that engages all the senses, the Sushi Fold slowly reveals a deliciously stylish contrivance within its wrapping. The fold achieves its color contrast by rolling one lighter colored napkin within a darker second napkin. The extra napkin can be used along with the first or be given to the guests as a keepsake. While the Sushi Fold obviously is a good fit for a meal of raw fish atop moist clumps of rice, it also works for any dining experience where the mood is refined and reserved. Fresh as a California roll and just as pleasing to the eye, the fold brings honor to any host.

**WASABI, GINGER?** Looking for all the world like *oshinko maki*—paper-thin seaweed encircling a bright burst of pink pickled daikon—the contrasting colors of the outer and inner napkins harmonize with the Zen-like place setting of rolled bamboo place mats and vividly colored tableware. The thin strip of rice paper that bundles the chopsticks can also serve as an offbeat place card. Expect *domo arigato* all around.

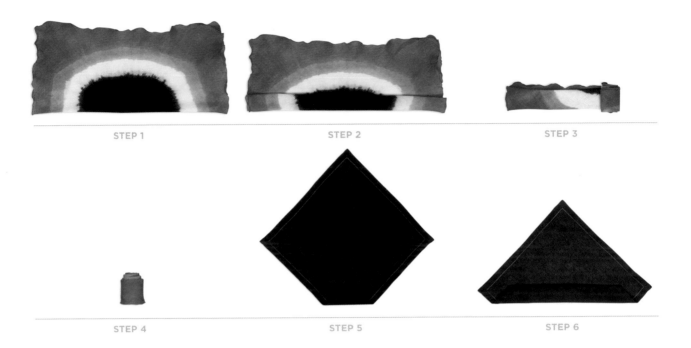

STEP 1    STEP 2    STEP 3

STEP 4    STEP 5    STEP 6

**NOTE:** This fold uses two different-colored napkins—one bright, one dark.

1. Begin with the brightly colored napkin (the inner roll) fully open, laid out as a square, then fold it in half with the folded edge on the bottom. Press.

2. Working from bottom to top, fold the napkin in 3-inch bands until you reach the top of the napkin. It's OK if there's a bit of cloth that extends above the final fold.

3. Beginning at one side of the band, roll up the napkin tightly.

4. When tightly wrapped, the top edges of the napkin are slightly askew, like a rosette.

5. Lay the second dark-colored napkin fully open, laid out in a diamond, and fold up 3 inches (measured from the bottom point).

6. Working from bottom to top, continue folding 3-inch bands until the entire napkin is a single band about 3 inches wide.

7. Flip the napkin over.

8. Place the first napkin roll on top of the left end of the second napkin approximately 3 inches from the end. The bottoms of both napkins should be evenly aligned, but the top of the inner napkin should extend a little above the outer one.

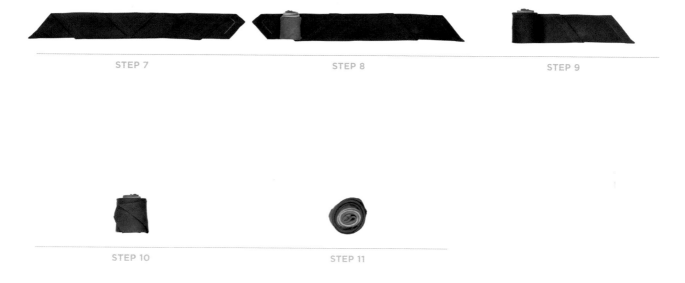

STEP 7 STEP 8 STEP 9

STEP 10 STEP 11

**9.** Lift the left end of the lower napkin and tightly roll it around the inner napkin, continuing to roll until you reach the other end, and being sure to keep the bottom of the roll even.

**10.** Tuck the remaining loose end into the folds of the outer roll.

**11.** Your slice of "sushi" can now be set upright.

## TABOO IN TOKYO

Table manners differ from culture to culture, but some things are consistent—pointing with utensils, for instance. Whether it's a spoon in Spain or a fork in Finland, don't point with dining implements. Likewise in Japan, where pointing with chopsticks is considered rude. But that's hardly the worst possible chopstick faux pas. Because chopsticks are used during Japanese funerals, there are two specific things you should NEVER do: 1. Never use your chopsticks to pass food to another person's chopsticks. This is how the remaining bones found among cremated ashes are passed between two family members. 2. Never leave your chopsticks sticking up in food. At the end of the cremation ceremony, this is how chopsticks are left in the ashes.

# On a Roll

## THE GIFT-ROLL FOLD

The British have a Christmas tradition of setting tables with "crackers," foil rolls tied at each end that are "cracked" open to reveal tiny gifts and candy. While the Gift-Roll Fold mimics the shape and utility of a cracker, it also serves as the napkin (and leaves no messy gift wrap at the table). But unlike crackers, this isn't just for holidays. Use it whenever you're in the mood to give your guests a gift, including weddings, showers, or other events. You don't have to include anything inside, but what fun is that? The gift can be as simple as an airline-size bottle of spirits or as refined as a treasured keepsake. Use various prints, patterns, and ribbons on the napkin to dress the place setting from country casual to uptown classic.

**DISCOVERING YOUR INNER GIFT:** The anticipation of a gourmet meal is heightened by the mystery of what guests might find inside their Gift-Roll Fold—any small item you tucked into the center of the napkin before rolling it. The demure polish of this navy-blue-and-white setting is balanced by the innate festivity of the napkin as gift, a pleasing gesture that cues guests that a celebration is in the making.

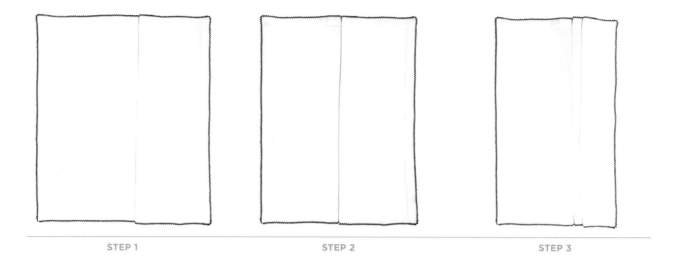

**ADDITIONAL MATERIALS NEEDED:**
ribbon, small gifts (optional),
scissors

1. Begin with the napkin fully open, laid out as a square, then visually note the vertical center of the napkin. Create a vertical pleat on the right side of the napkin by pinching a vertical fold about 3 inches right of center and then laying the pleat's folded edge on the center.

2. Repeat on the left side to make two panels that meet at the napkin's center. Press.

3. As in step 1, create a second vertical pleat on the left panel, laying the pleat's folded edge about 1 inch from the napkin's center.

4. Repeat step 3 to create a matching pleat on the right panel, laying the fold the same distance from the center as the pleat in the left panel. You now have the "casing" to wrap your gift. Press.

5. If you are including a gift (and you really should, you know), place it at the base of the napkin in the center. Starting at the bottom, roll the napkin up tightly and evenly around the gift.

6. Continue to roll up the napkin and gift, stopping about 4 inches before the top of the napkin.

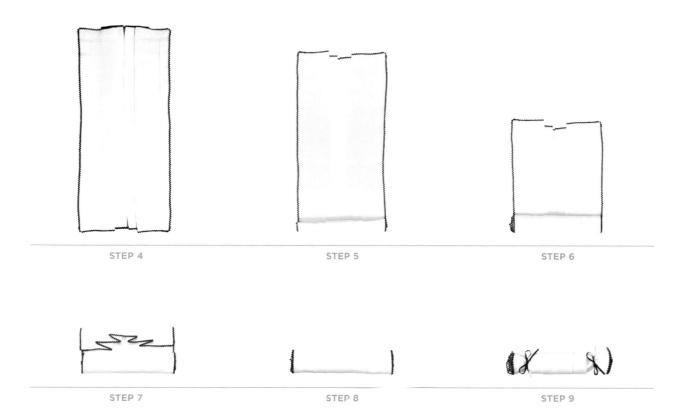

STEP 4                    STEP 5                  STEP 6

STEP 7                    STEP 8                  STEP 9

**7.** Fold the remaining top part of the napkin in half so that the top edge is now next to the roll.

**8.** Complete the roll.

**9.** Tie matching 12-inch-long pieces of ribbon about 2 inches from each end. *Message to dinner guests: Open me first.*

**THE FRILL OF IT ALL:** A contrasting scalloped edge is at once festive and urbane, trimming a Gift-Roll Fold with just a dusting of navy blue. A matching ribbon, the precise width of the embroidery, adds to the napkin's subdued air. Tied at each end with a casual bow, the narrow lengths of blue secure the goodie inside without ostentation.

# Birds of a Feather

## THE THANKSGIVING FOLD

Among the most celebrated meals in world history was a certain gathering in 1621 when American Indians and European newcomers broke bread together, a sterling example of an ideal where everyone is welcomed at the table. To welcome loved ones to your holiday table, the Thanksgiving Fold gives the peacock treatment to the holiday's bird of choice, the one Ben Franklin described as more savvy than the bald eagle could ever hope to be. Complemented with the natural curves of gourds or the more lighthearted shape of colorful corncobs (with cloves for eyes and almonds for beaks), the Thanksgiving Fold makes a turkey out of this easy fan fold.

**TURKEY SHOOT:** After guests retrieve their napkins, chargers and gourds are promptly removed to the kitchen or food staging area and later mulched. Thanksgiving is, after all, in gratitude to a harvest's bounty, so it's always appropriate to give something back to the earth.

| STEP 1 | STEP 2 | STEP 3 |

**ADDITIONAL MATERIALS NEEDED:**
slender-neck squashes or gourds
(see below), corn kernels, cloves,
nuts, corn husks, hot glue gun

**1.** Begin with the napkin fully open, laid out as a square, then fold it in
half vertically so that the fold is on the right. Press.

**2.** Create a horizontal pleat at the bottom by folding the napkin up
about 1½ inches from the bottom edge and folding it under itself.
Press.

**3.** Working from bottom to top, continue making pleats by alternating
folds, accordion style.

**4.** Stop folding when 4 to 5 inches remain at the top of the napkin.

**5.** Flip over the napkin.

**6.** Holding down the right side of the napkin, fold it in half.

**7.** Grasp the upper right corners (both layers) of the unpleated side
and diagonally fold down the right top corner as far as possible
(creating a triangle), tucking the corners deeply down into the pleats.
(The triangular fold creates a stand for the turkey's fanned tail.)

**8.** Grasp the triangle and stand it upright so that the pleats fall open
and form the turkey's fanned tail.

Shop for yellow squashes that have 1- or 2-inch stems, and then
glue on a finely shaped beak fashioned from a piece of corn husk.
Two cloves strategically placed behind a carefully cut gourd's stem
complete the illusion of the bird of the hour.

STEP 4

STEP 5

STEP 6

STEP 7

STEP 8

**WE CALL IT MAIZE:** Baby acorns serve as eyes and an unshelled almond makes a beak on a decorative corncob cut in half to stand upright on the plate. A piece of dark purple husk is first wrapped around the tip of the cob for the head and then eyes and beak are glued in place. Use a variety of items—nuts, corn kernels, dried beans—to decorate. Once guests take their seats, the cobs can be moved to the side of the plate to keep a watchful eye over the rest of the meal's proceedings.

**A GAGGLE OF GRACE:** A table full of chargers featuring yellow squash turkeys sets a surprisingly elegant tone (see photograph on pages 140–141). The napkins vary in shades of ocher, brown, and tawny, but all work together to continue the theme of fall, as does the rich sunflower centerpiece.

# SOURCES

ABC Carpet & Home
www.abchome.com

Anthropologie
www.anthropologie.com

April Cornell
www.aprilcornell.com

Barney's
www.barneys.com

Bed Bath & Beyond
www.bedbathandbeyond.com

Bergdorf Goodman
www.bergdorfgoodman.com

Bloomingdale's
www.bloomingdales.com

Cath Kidston
www.cathkidston.com

Crate & Barrel
www.crateandbarrel.com

Filene's Basement
www.filenesbasement.com

Fine Linens
www.finelinens.com

Fitzsu
www.fitzsu.com

Fred Segal
323-651-4129

French General
www.frenchgeneral.com

Gracious Home
www.gracioushome.com

Gracious Style
www.graciousstyle.com

Gump's
www.gumps.com

Hable Construction
www.hableconstruction.com

Hermes
www.usa.hermes.com

Horchow
www.horchow.com

Ikea
www.ikea.com

Kiitos Marimekko
www.kiitosmarimekko.com

Louis Boston
www.louisboston.com

Macy's
www.macys.com

Neiman Marcus
www.neimanmarcus.com

Pier 1 Imports
www.pier1.com

Pottery Barn
www.potterybarn.com

Restoration Hardware
www.restorationhardware.com

Saks Fifth Avenue
www.saksfifthavenue.com

Target
www.target.com

Urban Mercantile
www.urbanmercantile.com

West Elm
www.westelm.com

Williams-Sonoma
www.williams-sonoma.com

William-Wayne & Company
www.william-wayne.com

# ACKNOWLEDGMENTS

Many smart and talented people went with me on my journey to napkin land, and I am very thankful for their company and their hard and lovely work. I am so fortunate to have developed a fantastic rhythm (and friendship) with my regular collaborators: John Morse, a writer whose genius extrapolates the most fascinating tidbits of knowledge and humor from the most regular of subjects, and Mick Hales, a photographer of great finesse who casts such a beautiful and complex aura over something so simple and potentially mundane—a twenty-inch square of fabric.

I am especially indebted to a group of extremely talented individuals with whom I am blessed to work every day in planning and designing events all over the world. Truth be told, my studio conceived and produced this book as a *team,* and I am very proud of the results. Susie Montagna, Meg Gleason, Juliana Jaramillo, Siri Warren, Corrie Hogg, Natie Gutierrez, Caroline Wolfe, Incia Pleytez, Marco Mendez, Anne Feve Jones, Alyson Walder, Charo Figueroa, Jennifer Goebel, and Tracy Stedman—you created something very special. A big thank-you must be extended to the three incredible project managers in my office as well: Michelle Mutter, Christina Dimitriadis, and Niki Eways. Thank you for taking such great care of our clients, empowering me to throw myself into this endeavor.

My pals at Artisan: Ann Bramson, Ellice Goldstein, Deborah Weiss Geline, Nick Caruso, Barbara Peragine, Nancy Murray, Danielle Costa, and Jaime Harder share and work tirelessly to achieve the same goal—the best, most luscious books possible—and they never fail to deliver. Appreciation too to Arnold Katz Photography, which supplied the very helpful step-by-step photographs.

Someday I will write a proper love letter to my agent, Carla Glasser, but until then, I can't state enough how awesome she is. Thank you for taking such good care of me, Carla, and when that crazy artist side of me takes over too much, I appreciate your bringing me back down to earth.

There are many stores, designers, and artisans that I'd like to thank for their wonderful contributions to this book. Cheryl Kleinman created the gorgeous cupcakes on pages 47 and 49, and Mary Anne Wolfe scripted the elegant calligraphy throughout. New York City's ABC Carpet and Home, Global Table, Crate & Barrel, Clio, and Michael C. Fina provided us with the most exquisite tableware to complete our designs, and many of my pals and studio mates provided us with family heirlooms both precious and meaningful to layer our ideas with history. Thank you all.

Finally, it's been a big year of challenge and change for me, and I am grateful to have such a wonderful support system in my family and friends. Thank you Mom, Dad, Rob, Rachel, Lori, Marcia, Lolo, Robert, Diane, Yankito: I know this book is the precursor to so many good things to come.